Praise for *Seeds of Destruction*

"Hubbard and Navarro provide a cogent analysis of America's dangerous economic decline as well as a carefully thought out plan for recovery based on a manufacturing renaissance."

—**Clyde Prestowitz**, Founder and President
of the Economic Strategy Institute, and author
of *The Betrayal of American Prosperity*
and *Three Billion New Capitalists*

"A well-argued—and exceedingly timely—call to action for the White House and Congress to end partisan political bickering and move the American economy back to sound principles like free markets, entrepreneurship, and a renewed manufacturing base that will restore our nation's greatness. Hubbard and Navarro focus a bipartisan perspective on practical policy reform."

—**Larry M. Wortzel**, Ph.D., Commissioner
and former Chairman of the U.S.–China
Economic and Security Review Commission

"It is time for a clean sheet of paper that creates the ultimate focus on creating real jobs and driving the success of our private sector by significantly improving our global competitiveness and not further eroding it. Kudos to Glenn Hubbard and Peter Navarro for doing just that!"

—**Dan DiMicco**, Chairman, President,
and CEO, Nucor Corporation

"*Seeds of Destruction* is everything that Washington policymaking is not: sober, lucid, reasoned, timely, bipartisan, and constructive. The United States is on a path to greater danger and diminished aspirations. Hubbard and Navarro illuminate the path to fulfilling this generation's obligation to leave behind a nation with greater freedom and prosperity than it inherited."

—**Douglas Holtz-Eakin**, President of the American
Action Forum, and former Director of the
Congressional Budget Office (2003–2005)

Seeds of Destruction

WHY THE PATH TO ECONOMIC RUIN RUNS THROUGH WASHINGTON, AND HOW TO RECLAIM AMERICAN PROSPERITY

GLENN HUBBARD AND PETER NAVARRO

Vice President, Publisher: Tim Moore
Associate Publisher and Director of Marketing: Amy Neidlinger
Executive Editor: Jim Boyd
Editorial Assistant: Pamela Boland
Development Editor: Russ Hall
Operations Manager: Gina Kanouse
Senior Marketing Manager: Julie Phifer
Publicity Manager: Laura Czaja
Assistant Marketing Manager: Megan Colvin
Cover Designer: Alan Clements
Managing Editor: Kristy Hart
Project Editor: Anne Goebel
Copy Editor: Gayle Johnson
Proofreader: Williams Woods Publishing Services
Senior Indexer: Cheryl Lenser
Compositor: Nonie Ratcliff
Manufacturing Buyer: Dan Uhrig

This book is sold with the understanding that neither the author nor the publisher is engaged in rendering legal, accounting, or other professional services or advice by publishing this book. Each individual situation is unique. Thus, if legal or financial advice or other expert assistance is required in a specific situation, the services of a competent professional should be sought to ensure that the situation has been evaluated carefully and appropriately. The author and the publisher disclaim any liability, loss, or risk resulting directly or indirectly from the use or application of any of the contents of this book.

FT Press offers excellent discounts on this book when ordered in quantity for bulk purchases or special sales. For more information, please contact U.S. Corporate and Government Sales, 1-800-382-3419, corpsales@pearsontechgroup.com. For sales outside the U.S., please contact International Sales at international@pearson.com.

Company and product names mentioned herein are the trademarks or registered trademarks of their respective owners.

Printed in the United States of America

Second Printing October 2010

ISBN-10: 0-13-702773-7
ISBN-13: 978-0-13-702773-6

Pearson Education LTD.
Pearson Education Australia PTY, Limited
Pearson Education Singapore, Pte. Ltd.
Pearson Education North Asia, Ltd.
Pearson Education Canada, Ltd.
Pearson Educación de Mexico, S.A. de C.V.
Pearson Education—Japan
Pearson Education Malaysia, Pte. Ltd.

Library of Congress Cataloging-in-Publication Data:

Hubbard, R. Glenn.
  Seeds of destruction : why the path to economic ruin runs through Washington, and how to reclaim American prosperity / Glenn Hubbard, Peter Navarro. — 1st ed.
      p. cm.
  ISBN 978-0-13-702773-6 (alk. paper)
  1. United States—Economic policy—2009- 2. Free enterprise—United States. I. Navarro, Peter. II. Title.
  HC106.84.H83 2010
  330.973—dc22
                                    2010018952

To the youth of America—and their children.
We write this book in the hopes that, through sensible
and timely reforms, our generation will not impose
a crushing economic and tax burden on them.

Contents

Contents

Foreword

"Republicans want to go back and live in the 1950s. Democrats want to go back and work there."

That's the joke circulating about the American attitude toward our current economy, our past, and our prospects.

It's a short joke, but one that captures Americans' dark suspicions about our future. In the 1950s, jobs were available and pay was high. Americans found they were able to work fewer hours than before and buy better cars and appliances. Mortgages were low. Education was available and universities were good. The Midwest drew workers rather than sent them away. When someone lost a job, he found another. Teenagers went joyriding in their parents' cars. It all looked easy at the time. But today no one seems to be putting forward a plan that can take us to a 1950s level of broadly shared prosperity.

No one, that is, until these authors. In this dramatic nonpartisan book, Glenn Hubbard and Peter Navarro lay out the true roots of the current troubles. They then open their hands and show "seeds of prosperity," a new set of policies that can, if planted, make the economic garden grow even more dramatically than it did in the past.

No pair of authors is more qualified than these to undertake this. While he was Chairman of the Council of Economic Advisers at the White House in the early part of the nought decade, Glenn Hubbard wrote the soundest components in the 2001 and 2003 tax laws. As a scholar and dean of Columbia Business School, Hubbard has identified those changes in tax and regulatory law that can yield the most efficacious growth. Peter Navarro, a noted speaker and teacher, is author of numerous prescient and insightful books, including *The*

Coming China Wars, Always a Winner, and *What the Best MBAs Know.*

Hubbard and Navarro begin their work by laying out the aspects of the problem the rest of us can merely sense. In this decade, the economy has grown an average of 2.4 percent. That compares with an average of 3.2 percent in the period from 1946 to 1999. Employment is in trouble. After other downturns, American companies have been quick to rehire. Not this time. Workers are being rehired after the crash of 2007–2008, but at a dreary rate conforming more to European patterns than our own.

The authors also expose what might have been wrong in the assumptions about a decade like the 1950s. One is that strong unions can force the economy to grow by demanding high wages. The only thing that made the high-wage policy of the 1950s possible was that, back then, the United States had no international competitors. Europe was flat on its back amid its own rubble. Asia was a rice paddy. Today, the effect of a high-wage policy, whether instituted because of union pressure or because of pressure from the federal government, would be to drive employers overseas even faster than they are already going.

The authors then proceed to offer recommendations that appeal to simple common sense. The first is that the country begin to recognize something we have been ignoring: the importance of business and investment. To be sure, Americans pay lip service to the concept that the private sector matters. President Barack Obama has, for example, often said that the private employers will lead recovery. Yet we don't think about the fact that our tax structure holds those employers and investors back. The Internal Revenue Code currently punishes savings and investment relative to other economic activities. The bias also disadvantages us internationally. Other nations have long since recognized the importance of the corporate tax. They have cut rates, leaving our corporate tax one of the highest in the world.

A second step then would be to realign the tax code so that it moves into balance. The authors format an overhaul of the tax code that reduces capital gains taxes and other taxes on business and capital formation. Such a move sounds like it is "a gift for business," something some voters, having been laid off by business, are not inclined to make. But the effect of reducing taxes on capital will be to create new employers for ourselves and our children. Reducing taxes on capital also improves the quality of jobs that will be on offer. Instead of a future as a municipal official, a child will find a job with the next Google.

Giving capital its fair chance entails a third move—abolishing or curtailing the elements of the tax law written to favor the consumer above the producer. Such moves would include a reform that is hard to sell politically—a reduction in the home mortgage interest deduction. But the gift of the interest deduction is only precious because of the punishment the rest of the tax code metes out. In combination with lower tax rates and more jobs, ending the mortgage interest deduction will not hurt families. A balanced tax structure would, again, begin to channel money to where it is most productive—innovative projects and worthy investments.

The fourth major change the authors call for is that the country reject government as a manager of the business cycle. Our national habit of looking for federal help at signs of economic weakness has had a significant result: It has made government bigger. Today, as budget deficits mount, the federal government is rapidly moving toward 25 to 30 percent of the economy. That compares with the 20 percent that was the rule just a decade or so ago.

But our dependence on government has not given us what we were really asking for: strong growth. This is because, as the authors point out, reliance triggers a destructive dynamic. To finance our excessive government spending, the U.S. Treasury must issue substantial new debt. Foreigners and foreign governments like to lend to the United States. But the extent of our borrowing will eventually make us look risky. Though they may be lower now, interest rates will inevitably rise. Equally inevitably, higher rates will crowd out business investment. This crowding out in turn will decrease our ability to invest in essential functions such as defense, research, and education.

The last and final trouble is our trade deficit. As Hubbard and Navarro astutely illustrate, our trade imbalances are the result of several factors: that skewed tax system, which also puts exports at a disadvantage, our energy dependence, and those protectionist walls and deals that do exist already. It is time to set aside trade favoritism and develop constructive multilateral trade reform.

If these simple suggestions truly are "seeds of prosperity," why haven't others before Hubbard and Navarro recognized them? The first reason is the tendency of Congress and the White House to treat America like an emergency room. Next to other things it must manage—war, a Katrina, or a BP disaster—slowing growth does not look like an emergency. That slow growth, therefore, gets overlooked by politicians eager to play the hero by ministering to direr cases. Lawmakers' triage is understandable because crises have the rare capacity to catalyze our sluggish legislative bodies and voters into action. "Never waste a crisis," as Rahm Emanuel told an interviewer just after President Obama's election. But what the lawmakers forget is that even a gradual disease can be fatal. The sluggishness they despair of in their political conversations is a symptom of an economic slowdown.

There is a more profound reason for the American delay in addressing the causes of slow growth. In the postwar period, our textbooks have been called Keynesian, after the British economist John Maynard Keynes. Keynesianism, as it has been taught for the past half century, tends to neglect innovations, investments, and investors in favor of the consumer and shopper. Keynesianism likes the kind of growth it knows, home buying or factory work.

Keynesian principles have so penetrated our thinking that they determine our lexicon. When a television commentator tells viewers that consumer activity represents 70 percent of the economy—and the commentators do that often—the commentator is quantifying the economy using Keynesian measures. The very meters we trust to tell us how to invest are Keynesian—the Consumer Confidence Index, for example. Such meters are fine and good. But they do not capture producers' anxieties or hopes. When we hear that "strong jobs numbers may lead to inflation," the speaker is assuming, as Keynesians do, that there is always a trade off between unemployment and inflation. This is not the case. We have had decades with strong growth and low inflation, and we have had a decade where growth slowed and inflation took off. "Stagflation," the 1970s dynamic, is itself a contradiction of the Keynesian trade off.

Our national inability to see outside the Keynesian construct in fact contributed to the recent financial implosion. For decades, the message to Americans from politicians of both parties was that spending was good—especially spending on housing. The tax structure reinforced this first with that home mortgage interest deduction but then also with the numerous home credits available over the years for lower earners and tax-subsidized federal loans. Had Americans invested that money on new ideas and new companies, growth overall would have been stronger and more genuine. The exotic mortgages that vulnerable families began to sign up for were tacitly sanctioned by the rest of us out of the Keynesian habit of believing in housing.

Unfortunately, politicians from both parties seem these days content to muddle forward in Keynesian fashion. Due to budgeting rules, the tax codes that Hubbard coauthored are due to expire this year or next. The White House and many members of Congress have adopted a passive–aggressive approach to this process. Rather than extend the tax cuts, lawmakers and administration officials seem to be willing to let all or most of them expire. In addition, of course, Washington is blithely laying on new taxes, such as the health care planned 3.8 percent tax on so-called "unearned income." This last addition is itself a mighty burden, for it targets precisely those engines of growth described above. The result is to skew our tax system yet more against job creation. The total effect of the 2010 tax changes, even before any further increases are passed, is to impose the biggest tax increase on the country since World War II, and that in a time when the economy is still fragile. Lord Keynes himself, far wiser than today's Keynesians, would have been the first to point out the folly of that. In other words, at the present time, the United States truly is planting seeds of destruction, just as the title of this book suggests.

The good news is that scholars like Hubbard and Navarro do supply us with not only a new plan, but also a language for talking about that plan. Once voters can find the lexicon they need, they are ready to discuss, and eventually support, policies that will bring the progress for which we wax nostalgic. We will again enjoy that elusive thing that made the 1950s feel so good—not the union cards, not the music, not the lifestyle, but the growth.

—Amity Shlaes
Amity Shlaes is a Senior Fellow in Economic History at the Council on Foreign Relations, a Bloomberg columnist, and author of
The Forgotten Man: A New History of the Great Depression.

About the Authors

Glenn Hubbard is the Dean of the Graduate School of Business at Columbia University where he is also Russell L. Carson Professor of Finance and Economics. He served as Chairman of the President's Council of Economic Advisers from February 2001 to March 2003. During that time, he also chaired the Economic Policy Committee of the OECD.

Hubbard received his PhD in economics from Harvard University in 1983. He serves as a research associate at the National Bureau of Economic Research, on the Panel of Economic Advisors of the Federal Reserve Bank of New York, and as cochair of the Committee on Capital Markets Regulation. He also serves on the board of directors of ADP, Blackrock Closed-End Funds, KKR Financial Corporation, and Met Life. He is a regular commentator in the press, radio, and television.

Peter Navarro is a business professor at the University of California-Irvine. He has written numerous best-selling books on business strategy, economic forecasting, stock market investing, and public policy. These books include: *The Coming China Wars*, *The Well-Timed Strategy*, *If It's Raining in Brazil*, *Buy Starbucks*, *What the Best MBAs Know*, *The Policy Game*, *The Dimming of America*, and *Always a Winner*.

Navarro received his PhD in economics from Harvard University in 1986. His unique and internationally recognized expertise lies in his big picture application of a highly sophisticated—but easily accessible—macroeconomic analysis of the international business environment and financial markets for corporate executives, investors, and policymakers. He is a regular CNBC contributor and a widely sought-after and gifted public speaker who has appeared frequently on *Bloomberg TV* and radio, *CNN, NPR, ABC News, CBS News,* and *60 Minutes.*

Navarro's articles have appeared in a wide range of publications, from *BusinessWeek,* the *Los Angeles Times,* the *New York Times,* and the *Wall Street Journal* to *Harvard Business Review,* the *Sloan Management Review,* and the *Journal of Business.* He has also been interviewed on *60 Minutes.* His free weekly economic forecasting and investment newsletter is published at www.peternavarro.com.

The White House Plants Its Seeds of Destruction

If politics makes strange bedfellows, economics can sometimes make for a very odd couple. We are indeed two economists from two very different sides of the political aisle.

One of us—Glenn Hubbard—is a Republican who served as the Chairman of the Council of Economic Advisers for President George W. Bush during his first term. The other—Peter Navarro—is a Democrat who ran for Congress with President Bill Clinton's support.

The two of us met at Harvard University in the 1980s while working on our PhDs in economics. What we share now is a deep and abiding concern that the Obama administration has put into place a set of policies that ultimately contain the seeds of America's economic stagnation. And, as we argue, these seeds reflect the actions of both parties.

We fervently wish this were not so. In January 2009, both of us had high hopes for a young president seeking to give this fair nation a fresh start on a wide range of fronts. However, since taking office, President Barack Obama and his policy team have repeatedly stumbled across a surprisingly broad swath of issues and crises. The list of concerns that may be rightfully tacked upon the White House door is both long and alarming. It includes the following:

- The gross mismanagement of a massive fiscal stimulus that has created far more public debt than private-sector jobs.

- A historically unprecedented expansion of the powers—and balance sheet!—of the Federal Reserve that has raised many questions about future inflation concerns and regulatory overreach.

- An increasingly shrill tax policy that seems ever more interested in simply "soaking the rich" and punishing businesses rather than efficiently deploying our resources and balancing the federal budget.

- A misdirected energy policy that inexorably drags us deeper into our pernicious oil import dependence and likely dooms us to a dim future of soaring electricity and gasoline prices.

- A budget-busting health care bill that establishes unreasonable mandates, imposes heavy-handed insurance regulation, and serves up a massive new and grossly underfunded entitlement, all without adequately reining in out-of-control health care costs—and all in the name of progressive "reform."

- Last, a failure to confront our trading partners—particularly China—on a set of mercantilist and protectionist trade policies that have created chronic global trade imbalances and destroyed millions of American jobs while threatening the entire global free-trade system.

What is sorely missing from the Obama administration's "Seeds of Destruction" agenda is this critical realization: We as a nation cannot resolve what have become deep and systemic structural imbalances in our economy simply by throwing more and more money and more and more regulations and more and more taxes at the problem. Instead, the *real* key to long-term prosperity in America—and a secure national defense—lies first and foremost in restoring business investment and the entrepreneurship and technological innovation that come with it as the primary engine of growth and job creation.

As we will explain more fully in the first chapter, the economic growth of any nation is driven by only four components: consumption, business investment, government spending, and net exports. After more than a decade of economic stagnation spanning two asset bubbles, two stock market crashes, two recessions, chronic trade imbalances, and a bipartisan utter lack of both fiscal and monetary restraint, our "GDP Growth Driver equation" is, to put it in its most colloquial phrasing, totally out of whack.

We have saved too little and taxed too much, and thereby have significantly underinvested in the private sector—the most important engine of job creation in any economy. Meanwhile, soaring government expenditures are burdening our economy with massive budget deficits and the heavy burden of an equally massive public debt while chronic trade imbalances have siphoned off millions of potential jobs and depressed wages and income growth.

As a result, all four drivers of our GDP growth are out of structural balance and underperforming; it is hardly surprising that over the last decade our economy has grown far below its full employment rate. Indeed, given these structural imbalances, it's no surprise that millions of Americans are out of work and both wages and income remain depressed.

President Obama is certainly not to blame for all of this. Both political parties have made errors. And as Chapter 3 explains, the discretionary policy activism at the Fed helped spawn both the tech bubble of the late 1990s and the housing bubble of the last decade. In the process, the lack of monetary restraint and easy-money ways ushered in a decade of overconsumption and underinvestment, accommodating an almost total lack of fiscal restraint at the White House and on Capitol Hill.

Former President George W. Bush likewise must shoulder his fair share of the blame. He engineered passage of a budget-busting Medicare prescription drug benefit that further bloated an already out-of-control entitlements program, and that alone will add more than a trillion dollars to the deficit over the next decade. More broadly, this putatively fiscal conservative president allowed a wide range of other entitlement programs to grow on his watch.

Former President Bush may likewise be faulted for his handling of the beginning of the 2007–2009 recession and financial crisis. Although his administration was quick to apply a fiscal stimulus as the recession began in 2007, Bush's advisors mismanaged a series of corporate bailouts. At the same time, they were slow in addressing critical reforms in financial regulation that could have limited the spread and damage of the crisis.

Of course, the budget-busting policies from the Bush administration could not have been implemented without the support of a Congress far more concerned with pork barrel politics than long-term economic strategy. For example, the Bush administration's prescription drug bill passed with bipartisan support—despite its fiscal irresponsibility.

Although President Obama unquestionably inherited a very difficult economic situation from the Bush administration and a profligate Congress, he may rightly be blamed for making a very difficult situation far worse. As we will explain in this book, and as we noted a moment ago, virtually every policy that President Obama has adopted, or has sought to adopt, has perversely accentuated, rather than ameliorated, the American economy's pernicious structural imbalances.

Perhaps most egregious has been the Obama administration's radical expansion of the government sector at the same time the president has sought to significantly increase taxes on business investment and the private sector. This is but a fool's game that takes us further down the road of economic stagnation rather than toward the path of economic prosperity.

Equally egregious has been the role of a Democratic Congress in ratifying and, sometimes, as with the fiscal stimulus, even further perverting the Obama agenda. Indeed, just as former President Bush needed a Republican Congress to ratify some of his mistakes, so too has President Obama used a Democratic majority to push forward with an agenda that is counterproductive to long-term economic recovery. .

In large part because of the failures and foibles of White House policies, Congress has become highly polarized and quite clearly is unable to put the goals of national prosperity and security above its own petty, parochial politics. The beleaguered Democratic majority is desperately trying to hold on to its liberal base—even as its party splinters amid rancor and recriminations. Meanwhile, many Republicans, smelling blood in the water, seem far more intent on political posturing and regaining majority control than constructive policy reform.

What is missing from the national dialogue is any sense of urgency about America's long-term economic prospects. What both President Obama and congressional politicians on both sides of the aisle must realize is this: The greatest threat right now to America's national security is an economy too weak to support our national values and too structurally unbalanced to propel this nation to renewed strength and prosperity.

The difficult truth that must be told is that America is close to a destructive tipping point. We must change how we conduct our politics and economics and thereby rebuild and rebalance our economy, or we will inevitably go the way of all once-great nations and suffer an irreversible decline. This is the critical "Seeds of Destruction" road that we now find ourselves on—and it is a road that runs straight through Washington, DC.

However, America can follow a very clear path to long-term prosperity. Our Seeds of Prosperity blueprint is based on a set of sound economic principles that, over the course of American history, have helped make this country great. These principles include free markets and free trade; efficient taxation; a strong commitment to entrepreneurship, innovation, and technological change; a vibrant manufacturing base; and enlightened rather than heavy-handed regulation.

In setting forth our policy agenda, neither of us is a political Pollyanna. We understand that the destructive political equilibrium in which we have found ourselves will be difficult to transcend. However, we also understand that unless real change occurs in how this country conducts its politics, and unless we address the growth-killing structural imbalances in our economy, we as a nation will be unable to confront our challenges and seize the opportunities that lie before us—to the detriment of our children's future. That is why now is the time to find the appropriate path to prosperity and thereby achieve the economic security and political stability that come with such prosperity.

PART I

Getting from Seeds of Destruction to Seeds of Prosperity

What are the elements that drive any economy? What are the most important levers of growth to ensure long-term prosperity? The first two foundational chapters answer these questions by introducing the two analytical tools we will use to diagnose first and then offer appropriate policy fixes for the American economy.

The GDP Growth Drivers analysis discussed in Chapter 1, "America's Four Growth Drivers Stall and Our Economy Stagnates," makes it obvious that the American economy has been burdened with major structural imbalances in all four elements that drive economic growth. These structural imbalances, which include over-consumption, under-investment, excessive government spending, and chronic trade deficits, make it virtually impossible for our economy to grow at its full potential growth rate.

The Ten Levers of Growth analysis in Chapter 2, "How to Lift the American Economy with the Ten Levers of Growth," shows how America has lost its prosperous way by consistently ignoring so many of the principles that made it strong and great—from free markets and free trade to unfettered entrepreneurship, an unrivaled educational system, global-leading innovation, and a vibrant manufacturing base.

By ridding ourselves of the large structural imbalances in our economy and by taking much fuller advantage of the Ten Levers of Growth, we can move from the current "Seeds of Destruction" agenda to our Seeds of Prosperity policy blueprint.

America's Four Growth Drivers Stall and Our Economy Stagnates

"For most of the past 70 years, the U.S. economy has grown at a steady clip, generating perpetually higher incomes and wealth for American households. But since 2000, the story is starkly different. The past decade was the worst for the U.S. economy in modern times, a sharp reversal from a long period of prosperity that is leading economists and policymakers to fundamentally rethink the underpinnings of the nation's growth."

Washington Post (January 2010)[1]

America has the largest and most productive economy in the world. Yet something feels terribly wrong.

It's not just that millions of Americans remain out of work. It's also that income and wage growth have been stagnant for many for much of the last decade, while our job security seems far more uncertain and our job opportunities seem more limited.

Amid these labor market uncertainties, our capital markets have likewise been in crisis. It's not just that millions of American stock market investors have lost trillions of dollars. It's also that our faith in our financial markets and institutions has been shaken to the core—even as the financial crisis cost many innocent bystanders their jobs.

The past decade has been particularly unsettling for a generation of Americans raised on Wall Street's doctrine of "buy and hold." Indeed, our financial advisors assured us that all we had to do was buy and hold a portfolio of stocks representing the broad U.S. stock market, and we would have more than enough to retire on. Yet an American dollar invested in a mutual fund holding the Standard & Poor's 500 stock market index at the beginning of the appropriately named "nought decade" of the 2000s was worth only 90 cents at the end of the decade.

In these unsettling times, the central conundrum we now face is that America's once-robust and vibrant economy appears to many to depend on an unprecedented, massive, and totally unsustainable monetary and fiscal stimulus just to achieve modest growth rates and relatively small reductions in a persistently high unemployment rate. One very clear and present danger is that these massive stimuli—and the massive government debts that come with them—will force us down the road to confront very unpleasant choices and trade-offs among fiscal priorities ranging from education and national defense to Medicare, Social Security, homeland security, and the provision of critical infrastructure. These massive stimuli may also possibly reignite inflation in the midst of America's underperforming growth rate.

Under this cloud of uncertainty, the central policy question now facing the nation is this: How can America reharness the vibrant productivity growth of the private sector and resume its journey on the path of long-term prosperity? In order to answer this question—and thereby make things right—we first need a much better understanding of just what has gone wrong.

The first diagnostic tool we will use is the GDP Growth Drivers equation, which is a simple but very powerful representation of how all nations grow their economies. Using this diagnostic tool, we will see that after more than a decade of failure of our fiscal, monetary, and trade policies, the American economy has been saddled with major structural imbalances in all four of its growth drivers that are now stalling our economy. We as a nation are simply saving too little and therefore are investing too little in the primary engine of job creation—the private sector. We as a nation are also spending far too much of our wealth on government while chronic trade imbalances have left us severely weakened.

The GDP Growth Drivers Equation

The *Gross Domestic Product*, or GDP, is what economists use to measure the growth of any nation. The beauty and simplicity of the GDP Growth Drivers equation is that it illustrates that a nation's economic growth is driven by only four factors. It may be written like this:

GDP =
Consumption + Business investment + Government spending + Net exports

In this equation, "net exports" represents the difference between what a country exports to, and imports from, the rest of the world. It is important to understand up front that by the simple arithmetic of this equation, if a country such as the United States runs a trade deficit, its net exports will be negative, and its rate of GDP growth will be lower than it otherwise would be.

More broadly, using the construct of the GDP Growth Drivers equation allows us to very precisely diagnose why America is now facing a decade of slow growth and high unemployment. As we will see, all four American drivers of GDP growth have effectively run off the road—or, perhaps more accurately, been stalled by policy failures. Let's start our diagnosis, then, with a brief overview of the GDP itself.

GDP Growth Has Been Well Below Potential Growth

The 2007–2009 crash produced the worst recession since the Great Depression. However, the even bigger problem with the decade of the 2000s was that the U.S. economy performed well below its historical average and potential growth rate.

This concept of "potential growth rate" is particularly critical to both understanding and diagnosing America's economic woes. Any nation's potential growth rate (also called "potential output") measures the highest GDP growth rate a country can sustain over time without generating significant inflation. When the American GDP is growing at an annual rate consistent with its potential growth rate, our economy is creating as many jobs as it can in a sustainable fashion. However, if the American economy grows at a rate significantly below its potential growth rate for any sustained period of time, such as it did during the 2000s, millions of jobs that would otherwise be created are lost—and are very difficult to recover.

Exhibit 1.1 illustrates this problem of slow, below-potential growth by comparing the average annual, inflation-adjusted GDP growth rate during the 2000s to that of a historical benchmark based on the postwar period of 1946 to 1999.

Exhibit 1.1   The 2000s: A Decade of Underperformance

	Average Annual GDP Growth Rate
1946–1999	3.2%
2000–2009	2.4%

Source: Department of Commerce

During the benchmark period, the American economy grew at an average annual rate of 3.2%. What this benchmark number tells us with more than 50 years of data is that the potential growth rate of the American economy is achieved when the GDP grows a little over 3% a year.

What Exhibit 1.1 also tells us, however, is that during the nought decade of the 2000s, the American economy substantially underperformed that potential. It averaged a 2.4% GDP growth rate[2]—0.8% below the historical average.

You may think that a difference of only 0.8% in the GDP growth rate is a small number. However, this 0.8% gap makes an *enormous* difference in terms of the ability of the American economy to create new jobs and income growth.

The rough rule of thumb is that every 1 percentage point of GDP growth creates about a million jobs. This means that on a cumulative basis, a 0.8% underperformance in growth over the course of a decade translates to close to ten million jobs our economy failed to create. This is a stunning finding, because if we had created those jobs in the nought decade, the American economy would be much closer to full employment than it is today. If the American economy continues to perform well below its full potential growth rate, this will mean continued persistent high unemployment, downward pressure on wages and income, and a stagnant or perhaps even falling standard of living.

To understand why the American economy grew below its potential in the 2000s—and why it is likely to perform below its potential growth rate in this new decade unless something is done—we need to turn to our diagnosis of the ills afflicting each of the four GDP growth drivers.

To set up this diagnosis, look at Exhibit 1.2. It compares the percentage contributions of each of the four GDP growth drivers in our benchmark period of 1946 to 1999 to those contributions in the decade of the 2000s.

Exhibit 1.2 Structural Imbalances in the U.S. Economy Emerge in the Nought Decade

	1946–1999	2000–2009
Consumption	64%	70%
Business investment	16%	16%
Government spending	20%	19%
Net exports	0%	−5%

We first see that in the postwar period from 1946 to 1999, consumption expenditures accounted for an average of 64%, or just shy of two-thirds, of America's GDP growth rate. That's a share of the GDP that is consistent with most developed economies.

However, we also see that the share of consumption jumped significantly in the nought decade of the 2000s—specifically, to 70%. As we will discuss further, this is a signpost of America's overconsumption during that decade, which helped lead us first to a housing bubble and then to a housing bust.

The second statistical comparison that really leaps out from Exhibit 1.2 has to do with net exports. In our benchmark period from 1946 to 1999, American trade with the rest of the world had virtually no net negative impact on GDP growth—net exports were near 0%. However, during the 2000s, as our trade deficit more than doubled and grew to record proportions, the net negative impact of net exports on total annual GDP jumped to fully *minus* 5%. In doing so, this negative net export effect may have reduced our annual GDP growth rate by as much as half a percent—with the collateral loss in millions of jobs that might otherwise have been created.

As a final statistical comparison, Exhibit 1.2 shows that government expenditures as a percentage of GDP were actually slightly lower than the historical average during the nought decade. This means that at least during the nought decade, a bloated government sector does not appear to have been a significant brake on growth.

In this new decade, however, the problem we have going forward is a huge one.

As we will illustrate and discuss further, government expenditures are projected to zoom to as high as 30% of GDP under the impetus of massive fiscal and monetary stimuli and rapidly ballooning entitlement programs. Note particularly how the future projected deficits dwarf the current ones—which are historically large. Prospectively, the GDP Growth Driver equation therefore faces a significant worsening of its government spending problem—and a new and massive structural imbalance in its economy.

With these observations as background, let's turn to a more detailed analysis of each of the individual drivers of the GDP growth rate, starting with consumption.

The American Consumer's Roller Coaster

As previously shown in Exhibit 1.1, the American consumer is by far the largest driver in the GDP Growth Equation. In fact, in developed countries such as the United States, the European nations, and Japan, personal consumption expenditures typically account for fully two-thirds of economic activity. That's why a strong consumer with robust purchasing power is critical to any long-term American recovery.

Right now, the American consumer is anything but strong and robust. A large part of the problem is a frayed and tattered household "balance sheet" that remains as a leftover from overconsumption during much of the last decade. It was precisely this pattern of over-consumption (and a collateral low level of saving) that helped fuel America's housing bubble and eventually helped trigger the consumer-led 2007–2009 crash.

In fact, much of the overconsumption that occurred during the past decade was driven not by rising income and wages but rather by rapid home price appreciation. As housing prices rose during the bubble years, millions of Americans relied more and more on the black magic of mortgage refinancing for their spending needs rather than on rising wages and income.

By refinancing their mortgages and removing equity from their homes in the form of cash payouts, consumers effectively turned their homes into automatic teller machines. Collectively, this "house as an ATM" phenomenon provided a tremendous short-term consumption boost to the economy.

However, with consumers spending beyond their means and stretching their balance sheets, that kind of economic boom would inevitably go bust. Once the housing bubble burst, the "house as an ATM" consumption stimulus for the economy went into reverse, and consumption spending slowed dramatically.

Today, as the American economy attempts to resume its robust long-term growth pattern, a big brake on that growth remains a chastened consumer being squeezed on at least four fronts.

First, with housing prices stagnant and foreclosures an ongoing problem, the houses of many consumers are worth less than their mortgages. This "negative equity" problem puts a severe crimp on spending, and using one's home as an ATM is no longer an option.

Second, persistently high unemployment constrains future GDP growth in both an obvious and subtle way. Most obviously, all the people in unemployment lines, who aren't bringing home a paycheck, are by definition spending far less than they otherwise would. More subtly, a high unemployment rate puts strong downward pressure on the wages of those who are employed, further suppressing consumption.

In still a third dimension of the problem, inflation has vitiating effects on America's purchasing power. Not only are oil and gasoline prices in a long-term upward trend, but so are the prices of imported goods ranging from foreign cars to toys and electronics as the value of the American dollar declines.

Finally, income growth has actually been *negative* since the beginning of the nought decade—in contrast to very robust growth in the preceding two decades. This is illustrated in Exhibit 1.3 using one of the best measures of income growth—real, inflation-adjusted average median household income.

Exhibit 1.3   Real Median Household Income Over the Past Three Decades

Decade	Total Growth Rate for the Period	Average Annual Growth
1980–1989	18%	1.8%
1990–1999	16%	1.6%
2000–2008	−1.4%	−0.014%

You can see that during the 1980s, real median household income grew a total of 18% over the decade, or 1.8% annually. Similarly, during the 1990s, the total growth rate was 16%, or 1.6% annually. However, during the nought decade through 2008, income growth actually went negative—to a growth-vitiating *minus* 1.4% over the nine-year period.[3] As we shall explain, there are at least two reasons for this—one obvious and one more subtle.

The problem is not so much one of insufficient productivity growth, though an increasingly hostile tax, trade, and regulatory environment is harmful to income growth. A more subtle part of the problem, however, is rapidly rising health care costs. These out of control costs (which we squarely address in Chapter 9, "Why ObamaCare Makes Our Economy Sick") have taken an ever increasing share out of the total compensation paid to workers by employers in our employer-based health care system.

It follows from these observations that restoring the strength of the American consumer as an important driver of long-term economic growth is a complex and multidimensional task. Any broad rebalancing solution will incorporate at least five components.

First and foremost, it will mean putting unemployed Americans back to work. Second, it will mean stabilizing the housing market and housing prices. Third, it will mean more rapidly increasing the productivity of the American worker and making U.S. industry more competitive in international markets so that wage and income growth can once again boost purchasing power. Fourth, it will mean reducing America's dependence on increasingly expensive oil. Finally, it will mean creating a strong and stable dollar so that our import bill remains manageable.

*   *   *

Two final points on the consumption driver in the GDP Growth Driver equation are worth noting. First, nothing we have said about the falloff of consumer spending in this new decade should be construed as exhorting consumers to "go to the mall and help spend their way to prosperity." We tried that strategy in the 2000s, and what we got was initially a housing bubble, and then a housing bust, and then a bad balance sheet hangover.

Second, nothing we have said about the 2000s being a decade of overconsumption should be construed as an anticonsumption, moralistic judgment. Quite the contrary: We advocate a strong and robust consumer who generates sufficient income and wealth to enjoy a rising standard of living without going deeply into debt. Only with such a strong and robust consumer will we regain our path to prosperity.

Where Has All the Business Investment Gone?

Although consumption makes up more than two-thirds of America's GDP Growth Driver equation, business investment historically has accounted for a little over 15% of U.S. economic growth. What business investment lacks in size, however, it more than makes up for in volatility.

The recessionary fact of the matter is that business executives can reduce capital investment rapidly and thereby trigger a downturn. In fact, this is precisely what happened leading into the March 2001 investment-led recession.

One reason why business investment is so volatile has to do with what Depression-era economist John Maynard Keynes once called the "animal spirits" of entrepreneurs and business executives. At the first hint of recessionary trouble, executives often cut back on business investment—ironically sometimes making a recession a self-fulfilling prophecy.

Today, business investment in America has a lot more than a mere psychological problem. Since the 2001 recession, American business executives have chronically underinvested not just in new plants, equipment, and production facilities, but also in basic research and development (R&D).

Part of America's business investment problem has to do with the 2007–2009 crash and its aftermath. Since that crash, many businesses have continued to face a severe credit and liquidity problem. The paradox is that even as the federal government has driven down interest rates to near-zero levels, and even as the Federal Reserve has created over $1 trillion in new money, credit remains constrained—particularly for small businesses. Meanwhile, many households are still unable to obtain sufficient credit to purchase big-ticket, interest-rate-sensitive items such as houses and cars.

Not just a credit and liquidity problem plagues American businesses. With its mishandling of issues ranging from "cap and trade," health care reform, and tax hikes, the Obama administration has created tremendous uncertainty within the American business community—and attendant risk and uncertainty. The particularly dangerous nature of these "Seeds of Destruction" is this: In the presence of so much uncertainty and risk, business executives have been unable to accurately calculate projected rates of return on new investment. As a result, many corporations have invested less than they otherwise would. Combine this cloud of risk and uncertainty with a lack of access to credit, and you wind up with the financial equivalent of a black hole that sucks the life out of domestic business investment.

It would be a big mistake, however, to assume that the lack of adequate business investment in America is simply a short-term problem driven by a lack of adequate credit and liquidity and rising uncertainty over regulatory and tax policies. This continued "sand and grit" in America's financial system certainly helps account for the short-term, cyclical downtrend in business investment during the 2007–2009 crash. However, the harsh reality we must also confront is that domestic business investment in new industrial capacity has been in a longer-term decline since at least 2001.

A big part of the problem, as evidenced by the falloff in industrial production and the loss of six million manufacturing jobs during the nought decade, is the phenomenon of offshoring. Over much of the past decade and continuing into this new decade, American business executives have increasingly chosen to transfer much of their production, along with much of their R&D and many of their other operations, to foreign countries.

Debates over offshoring and its possible negative effects on domestic investment and growth in America make it tempting to blame the rise of free trade and wave the bloody shirt of "cheap foreign labor." Such an explanation, however, is far too simplistic. As we will explain in the next chapter when we discuss our Ten Levers of Growth, free trade is an essential component of global economic growth and stability.

The real problem American business executives face is not free trade *per se*. Rather, it is that in today's global marketplace, American corporations often fight the free-trade wars with both hands tied behind their backs.

One hand is tied behind the backs of American business executives because of the greater regulatory and tax burdens that are imposed on American soil relative to the burdens competitors face in other countries.

The second hand which is tied behind the backs of American business executives relates to the tendency of several of our key trading partners to engage in both mercantilist and protectionist policies that make it almost impossible for American companies operating on American soil to compete freely and fairly.

Accordingly, increasing business investment again in America will require a comprehensive overhaul of three critical policy areas: regulation, tax, and trade.

There's Too Much Government Spending

Let's stop now and take stock of where we are so far in this chapter. We know that two major constraints on America's long-term economic recovery are overconsumption in the consumption driver of the GDP Growth Driver equation and underinvestment in the business investment driver.

21

The third major constraint on America's long-term economic recovery presents us with a seeming paradox. That constraint is *overspending* by the federal government.

We saw in Exhibit 1.2 that excess government spending was not a significant constraint on GDP growth throughout much of the nought decade. The problem lay more in structural imbalances in the consumption, business investment, and net exports growth drivers.

This current decade, however, is likely to witness explosive and sustained growth in government expenditures. That such overspending by the federal government might actually slow down America's growth prospects would seem to be a paradox, because according to the GDP Growth Driver equation, if government spending goes up, so must the GDP.

That "stimulus effect" may be true in the short run. However, over the longer term, large and chronic budget deficits represent one of the worst seeds of economic stagnation that any White House and Congress can plant because of their negative impacts on all three *other* drivers in the GDP growth equation. Before we come to understand why this harm is done, let's take a further look at the deficit and public debt numbers.

Exhibit 1.4 compares the actual budget deficits run in the 2000s to the projected budget deficit picture in the 2010s. In reviewing this exhibit, it is important first to understand that the deficits that occurred during the Bush administration, particularly during the second term of George W. Bush, were historically large in absolute terms. That said, you can see that the Obama deficits projected by the CBO dwarf the Bush deficits.

There are several reasons why the Obama deficits are likely to significantly choke growth—and why the CBO estimates that America's real GDP will grow by only 2.4% annually from 2015 to 2020 once the stimulus effects wear off.

Exhibit 1.4   The Daunting Budget Deficits of Our Future

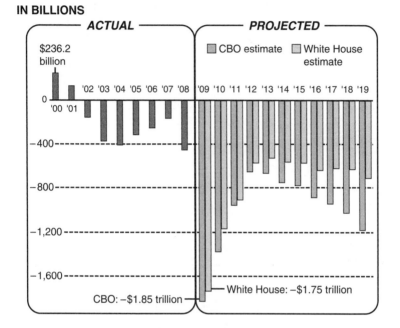

The first reason is the simplest to understand. A rapidly rising debt burden for the federal government means that more and more of our tax dollars must be paid to service interest on that debt. With foreigners holding over half of our public debt not held by the Federal Reserve and other government institutions, payments on debt flow right out of America and right out of the GDP Growth Driver equation.

The second problem is slightly more complex. It has to do with how America's budget deficits are actually financed—and whether the financing instrument chosen will be either inflationary or contractionary.

To finance its budget deficits, the American government has two basic options. It can either raise taxes or sell U.S. Treasury bonds. If the Obama administration raises taxes, as it has shown a propensity to do, that will be contractionary for the economy. This is because higher taxes take money out of consumer pocketbooks and thereby reduce consumption in the GDP Growth Driver equation. Higher taxes also take money out of corporate budgets that might otherwise be used to invest in new plants, equipment, and facilities.

Alternatively, if the Obama administration chooses to sell Treasury bonds to finance its deficits, the ultimate effect will be either higher interest rates or higher inflation—depending on who actually buys the bonds.

One possible bond buyer is the general public. In this financing scenario, the Treasury Department sells the bonds on the open market. However, in order to do so, the Treasury Department typically must offer higher interest rates on its bonds as the economy recovers. These higher interest rates, in turn, spill over into the corporate bond market.

In this way, the higher interest rates caused by deficit spending are said to "crowd out" business investment in the GDP Growth Driver equation, thereby slowing down GDP growth.

If the Treasury Department wants to avoid this crowding-out effect, it can sell its bonds to another possible buyer instead—the U.S. Federal Reserve. This type of deficit financing is called Fed "accommodation," and it happens when the Fed is willing to buy the Treasury bonds before they are put on the open market at the prevailing interest rate.

The problem with this type of bond financing and "Fed accommodation" is that it is inflationary. Inflation occurs because the Federal Reserve is simply printing new money to buy the bonds.

Of course, once inflation begins to rise rapidly, the Fed must raise interest rates to control inflation. At this point, you get the same growth-killing, crowding-out effect on business investment as well as on consumer spending for interest-rate-sensitive, big-ticket items such as houses and autos.

The bottom line of this diagnosis is a lesson apparently not understood by the Obama administration. Massive budget deficits are totally incompatible with long-term economic recovery. By definition, they plant some of the most potent seeds of economic destruction of any government policy—higher taxes, higher interest rates, and higher inflation.

Net Exports Are a Net Negative

In an age of globalization and in an increasingly flat world, the long-term growth rate of any nation's economy often is ultimately determined by the strength or weakness of a country's net exports—the difference between what a country sells to the rest of the world and what it buys.

On the plus side, a nation's exports make a positive contribution to economic growth by creating domestic jobs. On the negative side, however, when the United States buys foreign oil from countries such as Saudi Arabia and Venezuela or foreign steel or electronic goods from countries such as Germany and China, these other countries enjoy the benefits of increased jobs, wages, and GDP growth.

Of course, when a country such as the United States imports more than it exports, it is running a trade deficit, and its net exports are negative in the GDP Growth Driver equation. That's precisely the problem we observed in Exhibit 1.1. Although America kept its trade balance at close to even throughout much of the postwar period leading up to 2000, it has run significantly larger trade deficits since the beginning of the nought decade. By the simple arithmetic of the GDP growth equation—and like a crooked college hoopster—these negative net exports shave critical growth points off America's economic growth rate.

To be clear, we're not implying that imports *per se* are in any way negative for a nation. Imported goods provide consumers with much more choice while helping lower prices in markets around the world. Rather, the problem comes when America runs large trade deficits over a much extended period.

In fact, America's chronic deficits have three primary sources. The first is the anticompetitive nature of our corporate tax system. Not only must American exporters contend with the second-highest corporate tax burden of all the major economies in the world, but they also face a "double taxation" on anything they earn abroad.

The second source of America's trade deficits is what former President George W. Bush once called America's addiction to foreign oil. America depends on foreign oil imports for over half of its oil needs, and America's petroleum import bill accounts for over 40% of the total U.S. trade deficit.

These expenditures on foreign oil effectively act as a "tax" on both American consumers and American businesses. When American consumers pay more to foreign oil producers to heat their homes and fill their gas tanks, that's money lost that could otherwise go into driving the domestic economy. By the same token, when American businesses pay more for their energy needs, this drives up production costs, reduces the competitiveness of American businesses, and leads to lower output and fewer jobs.

The third source of America's chronic trade deficits is the mercantilist and protectionist trade policies of our major trading partners—particularly our largest trading partner, China. This has resulted in a related structural imbalance between savings and consumption, in which Asia saves too much and the United States consumes too much.

Reducing the U.S.–China trade and savings imbalances is particularly important in America's long-term economic recovery. This is because Chinese exports to the United States constitute fully 45% of America's trade deficit and 75% when petroleum imports are excluded.

Conclusion

This chapter has used the GDP Growth Driver equation to diagnose a variety of ills afflicting the four drivers of America's economic growth—consumption, investment, government spending, and net exports. Our diagnosis tells us that we face yet another decade of slow growth and high unemployment if we continue down the path of a low savings rate and lack of adequate business investment coupled with too much government spending and large and chronic trade deficits.

The next chapter introduces the Ten Levers of Growth to explore more fully how we can turn around the sluggish American economy. In this way, we will finish building the foundation for our Seeds of Prosperity analysis and policy blueprint.

Endnotes

1. Neil Irwin, "Aughts were a lost decade for U.S. economy, workers," *Washington Post* (January 2, 2010), http://www.washingtonpost.com/wp-dyn/content/article/2010/01/01/AR2010010101196.html.

2. Omits last quarter of 2009, which was unavailable at the time of this writing.

3. At the time of this writing, the Bureau of Labor Statistics only provided data through 2008.

chapter two

How to Lift the American Economy with the Ten Levers of Growth

---

"Give me a lever long enough and a place to stand, and I will move the world."

Archimedes, 230 B.C.

How can America regain its robust rate of economic development and growth and thereby resume its journey on the path toward long-term prosperity? A very big part of the answer may be found in the Ten Levers of Growth that have emerged from several centuries of economic history, thought, and research results.

Lever One: Free Markets Free of Corruption and Monopoly Best Promote Growth

In our support of the free market as the central engine of American growth, we offer neither a conservative political argument nor naive Panglossian economics. In the spirit of Winston Churchill, who once observed that "democracy is the worst form of government except all those other forms that have been tried," we are fully aware that free-market capitalism can be a very messy affair full of flaws, foibles, and market failures.

An obvious case in point from the 2007–2009 crash is the role of the free market in creating a housing bubble that would eventually go bust—almost bringing our credit and banking system to its knees. In a frenzy of speculation, real estate appraisers inflated home values to qualify consumers for mortgages they couldn't afford, lending institutions were more than happy to write mortgages that would likely lead to foreclosure, large financial institutions grossly underestimated the risks of speculating in mortgage-backed securities—and so the sad and sordid story went.

These market abuses notwithstanding, in his landmark 1776 book *The Wealth of Nations*, the economist Adam Smith, father of modern economics, identified this undeniable truth: A free market free of monopoly elements must inevitably be the best mechanism to promote economic growth. In a competitive free market, self-interested individuals will invariably invest any given resource—land, labor, or capital—so as to earn the highest possible return on it. Through the power of Smith's famous "invisible hand," a nation's resources will be allocated most efficiently, and its economy will therefore enjoy its most robust growth.

The centrally planned economy of the Soviet Union ignored this basic truth and collapsed. The fastest-growing economy over the past three decades, that of China, did not realize its enormous potential until its leaders privatized many of China's state enterprises and unleashed the power of private enterprise.

The challenge now facing America after the 2007–2009 crash is to fix our free-market system without crippling—or cutting off—the powerful invisible hand of our markets. Regrettably, as we will illustrate throughout this book, the Obama administration is not meeting this challenge. Rather than fixing the flaws of the marketplace with a light hand and laser-targeted reforms, Obamanomics is smothering our markets with layer upon layer of needless and counterproductive taxes and regulations, thereby substituting government failure for the free market's failings.

Lever Two: Free and Fair Trade Helps All Countries Grow

Just as we are realists about the power of the free market, so too are our eyes wide open on the question of whether free trade always benefits all nations. The "gains from free trade" argument was originally set forth by one of Adam Smith's contemporaries, David Ricardo.

Consider a Ricardian world that has only two countries, neither of which trades with the other. If these two autarkic countries enter into free trade, neither country has to produce everything each of them needs. Instead, each country can specialize according to its own "comparative advantage." In other words, each country specializes in what it does best.

Through this process of specialization based on comparative advantage, each country then benefits from a greater division of labor and greater economies of scale and, in doing so, uses its resources more efficiently. The result is a higher level of total production and job growth in the two countries combined than would exist in a state of autarky.

It is particularly ironic given today's sad state of America's trade relations with its most important trading partner—China—that in promoting the doctrine of free trade several centuries ago, Ricardo faced his stiffest opposition from the so-called "mercantilists." Mercantilism was the prevailing economic theory of the sixteenth through eighteenth centuries. The mercantilists believed that any nation's wealth could be measured by how much gold and silver bullion it possessed.

Under the banner of mercantilism, countries ranging from England and France to the Netherlands, Prussia, and Spain sought to accumulate as much bullion and trade surpluses as possible by using a combination of tariffs to protect their own markets and subsidies to promote their exports. Of course, the results of these "beggar thy neighbor" policies more often were war and turmoil rather than economic prosperity.

It would be Adam Smith, not Ricardo, who would eventually put the final intellectual dagger through the heart of mercantilism. Smith astutely observed that a nation's productive capacity—its machinery and labor and not its gold and silver and trade surpluses—was the real source of growth and measure of prosperity.

The broader message for these modern times of this now centuries old "mercantilist" debate is that free trade between two nations will never lead to stronger economic growth for both countries unless *both* play by the rules. That means free trade must also be fair trade so that neither country can protect its markets from the other or engage in mercantilist practices such as currency manipulation or the use of export subsidies to promote its exports at the expense of the other.

Unfortunately, one of the biggest obstacles to America's long-term prosperity is its free-trade battle with a mercantilist and protectionist China. Regrettably, the Obama administration has refused to engage China constructively on a set of trade reforms that would be beneficial to both countries. That's why trade reform aimed at restoring the powers of a global free-trade regime will feature prominently in our policy blueprint.

Lever Three: Entrepreneurship Is the Linchpin of Long-Term Growth

The greatest intangibles of America's economic greatness, over its long economic history, have been the creativity and innovative spirit of its entrepreneurs. It was an Austrian economist residing at Harvard who, in 1942, first formally explained the powerful catalytic role of entrepreneurship in promoting growth.

In his 1942 treatise *Capitalism, Socialism, and Democracy*, Joseph Schumpeter described a "gale of creative destruction" in which new products would continually drive older products out of the marketplace—and often drive the firms that produced those obsolete products out of business. In this competitive storm, the horse-drawn carriage gives way to the automobile, the typewriter gives way to the word processor, the VHS cassette tape gives way to the DVD, the phonograph yields to the iPod, and so on.

To Schumpeter, at the center of this gale of creative destruction is the entrepreneur who reforms or revolutionizes the production process by producing old products in new ways or by using new technologies to produce entirely new products. Like Adam Smith, Schumpeter understood that the profits an entrepreneur hopes to earn provide the incentive for bringing together the factors of production to start new firms and to innovate with new goods and services. In Schumpeter's protean world, only by unleashing the power of entrepreneurship will the process of growth continue.

Regrettably, Obamanomics is not creating an atmosphere conducive to entrepreneurship. Whether it be through the introduction of onerous taxes and wage controls or the micromanagement of bailed-out corporations, the Obama version of Uncle Sam is acting far more like Big Brother of dinosaurs than a Schumpeterian enabler of growth.

Lever Four: Without Savings, There Can Be No Investment and Growth

To grow, economies must produce. To produce, economies must invest in physical productive capital such as machines, computers, and tools. However, as economists such as Sir Roy Harrod and Evsey Domar have observed, sustained investment in productive capital requires savings. Indeed, one of the ironclad laws of economics is that over time, saving must equal investment.

Of course, the policy challenge for any nation is to balance its consumption with its investment needs. If a nation saves too little, it grows too slowly. If it saves too much, its current generations must sacrifice too much consumption in order to provide robust growth over time for future generations.

In 1961, Nobel Laureate, economist, and Columbia professor Edmund Phelps proposed solving this intergenerational problem through the application of his "Golden Rule." To find the appropriate intergenerational balance between current and future generations, a nation's current citizens should do unto future generations as this current generation would have future generations do unto them.

Although Phelps' Golden Rule has theoretical appeal, it offers little guidance as to what exactly America's "optimal" savings rate should be. Nonetheless, we can state with a high degree of confidence that at least over the course of the past decade, America has systematically run roughshod over Phelps' Golden Rule by overconsuming and underinvesting as a nation—thereby burdening future generations with a huge debt.

It follows from these observations that one of the most critical elements of our policy blueprint will be to find ways to boost the American savings rate—and therefore investment. This savings rate boost will inevitably require a reform of our tax policies toward saving.

It also will require bold reforms regarding the funding and administration of various entitlement programs that now account for a large and increasing share of the federal budget.

Lever Five: Without a Stable Banking System and Strong Financial Markets, Savings Can't Be Transformed into Investment

The need for a nation to save in order to grow is not the end of the capital investment story; it's just the beginning. In order for firms to invest in factories, machinery, and computers, they must have access to the funds to do so.

At least some of this funding can come from a firm's "retained earnings." Retained earnings are simply the profits that are reinvested in the firm rather than taken out to pay the firm's owners.

For many firms, however, retained earnings are insufficient to finance the rapid expansion required to fuel high rates of economic growth. That's why, as a practical matter, most firms, particularly larger ones, acquire the financial capital needed to grow from two other sources: the banking system, which provides loans, and the financial markets, which allow firms to raise capital by issuing new stock shares and bonds. Together, the banking system and financial markets act as intermediaries for the savings that households accumulate.

If the banking system breaks down, so does the availability of credit and liquidity. Of course, when credit dries up, so does the capital investment necessary to drive growth. Such a breakdown and collateral credit crunch is what helped bring both the U.S. economy and the broader global economy to the brink of collapse during the depths of the 2007–2009 crash.

By the same token, if a country's stock and bond markets break down—or investors lose confidence in those markets—a similar blow occurs to the availability of credit and liquidity. For example, when the stock market is in a prolonged downward trend, companies are reluctant to issue new shares to raise capital for investment. This is true because they receive only "bargain basement" prices that dilute the value of existing shares and drive their stock price even lower.

Right now, our banking system and financial markets are far less stable than they need to be in order to accommodate America's economic recovery. The sad irony is that the threat to these institutions no longer comes from the 2007–2009 crash itself. Rather, it comes from a gaggle of Obama administration post-crash "reforms" and regulatory changes that seem far more likely to choke the flow of capital rather than help it flow freely.

Lever Six: Innovation and Technological Change Matter More Than Machines and Workers

Although capital investment is critical to fueling growth, growth is far more than a simple story about providing more and more machinery and equipment to the workforce. In fact, one of the most interesting paradoxes of economics is this: If you simply keep adding more physical capital to the workforce, eventually you will reach a point where growth becomes stagnant.

Economies can fall into such a "steady state" or stagnant growth trap because of the "law of diminishing returns." Intuitively, if a business provides more and more machines to a fixed number of workers, the incremental benefit of each new machine to production must inevitably decrease. Over an entire economy, these diminishing returns eventually constrain growth to a stagnant steady state.

In 1956, Nobel Laureate and MIT professor Robert Solow first formalized this problem. Solow's growth model also showed us that the only way to break the bonds of steady-state stagnation is through rapid innovation and technological change that lift the productivity of both capital and labor out of the steady state.

Just what do we mean by technological change? Much of such change involves using new and improved machines that do the job better than existing ones. However, significant technological change can also take place by managerially changing the manner in which production takes place.

A shining example of managerial-driven technological change is Toyota's pioneering just-in-time inventory system, which revolutionized the auto industry. With this system, the parts involved in automobile assembly arrive at the factory at the exact time they are needed. That means fewer workers are needed to store and keep track of parts in the factory, so the quantity of goods produced per hour worked increases.

Regardless of which type of technological change we are talking about, in the long run, Solow's lasting insight is that such change is ultimately more important to the growth rate than the amount of capital and labor used in the production process.

Although America has always been at the forefront of innovation and technological change in the world, one of the big problems now facing us is that more and more of our country's R&D is being offshored. Such R&D represents the seed corn of technological change and innovation—and other countries are now eating ours. A root cause of this problem is a set of trade and tax policies that discourage domestic investment and a set of protectionist policies by our trading partners that force American companies to locate both production and R&D facilities overseas.

Lever Seven: "Human Capital" Matters as Much as Physical Capital

Thus far, we have highlighted the importance in the production process of savings and investment, physical capital such as machinery and equipment, and technological change. Although all of these elements are critical, it may ultimately be the quality of the American workforce that will provide us with our greatest competitive advantage and our most sustainable rates of growth.

In 1964, University of Chicago economist and Nobel Laureate Gary Becker was the first to really focus on, and formalize, the concept of "human capital." In Becker's world, human capital is the accumulated knowledge and skills that workers acquire from education and training as well as from their life experiences. As workers increase their human capital, their productivity also increases. Therefore, by boosting the education, training, and skill levels of a country's workforce, Becker persuasively argued, a nation's workforce can become much more productive with any given stock of capital.

From a long-term growth perspective, the big bonus associated with higher worker productivity is not just the production of more goods and services with a given number of resources. Rising productivity also leads to rising wages, more purchasing power for consumers, and an even stronger spur to growth. Indeed, as the GDP Growth Driver analysis has taught us, a steady rise in income is an integral part of the long-term growth process—one that has been conspicuous in its absence for many over the decade as income growth has stalled.

In addition, it is worth noting that the relevance of human capital to economic growth—and the need for any nation to invest in its education and training system—has taken on even more importance. In this era, advanced skills and information technology services increasingly drive production processes. Despite this importance, we are seeing our educational system—particularly our higher education system, which is the envy of the world—bearing the brunt of America's economic stagnation as state budgets are squeezed.

Lever Eight: Oil Price Shocks Stunt the Growth of Oil-Import-Dependent Nations

Since World War II, every recession suffered by the American economy has been preceded by a significant oil price shock. Although there is some academic debate about whether oil price shocks actually precipitated those recessions, a wealth of academic studies conclusively show that the growth of heavily oil-import-dependent nations such as the United States is highly vulnerable to rising oil prices.

It is certainly no mystery why oil price shocks and, more generally, rising oil prices lead to slower economic growth. In fact, any oil-import-dependent economy will suffer from both supply-side and demand-side effects that will lower production output, reduce employment, and slow down the economy.

On the supply side, crude oil is an important input for many companies. Consequently, any increase in the price of oil leads to a rise in production costs. This linkage is particularly true for heavy manufacturing industries such as chemicals and plastics, which use oil directly in the production process rather than simply as a source of energy. Rising production costs, in turn, lead to lower output, fewer jobs, and falling revenues.

On the demand side, rising oil and gasoline prices act as a pernicious "foreign tax" on consumers. Instead of paying $30 to fill their gas tanks, consumers may pay $60 to travel the same number of miles.

The extra $30 that flows out of the country into the coffers of the OPEC oil cartel is money that otherwise could have been spent in the domestic economy to the benefit of American businesses and workers.

It should be clear from these negative supply-and-demand effects that rising oil prices act as a brake on two of the key drivers in the GDP Growth Driver equation—consumption falters through a loss of purchasing power, and business investment is hurt by higher costs. This is not the end of the growth-stalling story, however. Because oil imports constitute more than 40% of the U.S. trade deficit, rising oil prices also help put the brakes on a third growth driver in the GDP equation—net exports.

For all these reasons, it is critical that America reduce its dependence on foreign oil. To these reasons we add one more: Many energy economists now believe that rapidly rising oil demand from emergent countries such as China and India, coupled with an increasingly constrained oil supply, will lead to a steady rise in world oil prices. If these economists are correct, such a sustained oil price shock would have the same kind of effect on America's long-term growth prospects as a python has on its victims as it tightens it grip.

Lever Nine: A Healthy Nation Is a Productive and Prosperous Nation

During the intense and often partisan debate over the Obama health care bill in 2010, proponents of the bill frequently argued that improved health care coverage and delivery would help promote economic growth in America. In fact, considerable research supports this argument.

For example, University of Chicago professor and Nobel Laureate Robert Fogel has highlighted the close connection between economic growth and improvements in human physiology. In the simplest terms, as people become taller, stronger, and less susceptible to disease, they also become more productive. The lack of proper nutrition in some countries can also affect intelligence levels, often permanently. Fogel's conclusion is that a critical link exists between the health of the population and the rate of its economic growth.

Although this is a good argument to support health care reform, good arguments should never be used to support bad legislation. As we explain more fully in Chapter 9, "Why ObamaCare Makes Our Economy Sick," the Obama health care plan relies on heavy-handed mandates, invasive regulations, and unaffordable new entitlements. It will do little to address the most critical problem with health care—rising costs.

Lever Ten: A Solid Manufacturing Base Makes for a Strong Economy

No matter how many trillions of dollars in fiscal stimulus, easy money, and massive deficit spending President Obama throws at the American economy, a long-term economic recovery needs a revitalization of America's manufacturing base. Therefore, although a strong manufacturing base may be our tenth and last lever of economic growth, it is hardly our least.

Manufacturing jobs are critical to a strong economy for at least three reasons. First, manufacturing jobs create more growth in other sectors—a critical factor with our unemployment rate remaining stubbornly high. This "output multiplier" effect is supported by the observation that for every dollar of final manufacturing output, America creates almost a dollar and a half in related services such as construction, finance, and transportation.

Manufacturing jobs also tend to enjoy a "wage premium." For example, as one MIT study noted, manufacturing jobs pay significantly higher wages than jobs in other sectors; and this wage premium is evident across the educational spectrum. This study also found that the wage premium is higher still for female workers.[1]

Third, in an important synergistic effect with our sixth growth lever, a strong manufacturing base spurs the technological innovation necessary to boost productivity, wage growth, and consumer purchasing power. Manufacturing is critical because the innovation process is primarily driven by R&D expenditures. In fact, U.S.-based manufacturers account for fully two-thirds of all private R&D in America. This manufacturing-based R&D leads to a ripple effect that creates new products, more production, additional jobs, higher productivity, and more wealth.

The importance of manufacturing and industry is reinforced by a historical view of the growth process and the endemic poverty that existed before the Industrial Revolution in the 1700s. In fact, prior to 1300 A.D., no sustained increases in real economic growth per capita occurred—only subsistence living prevailed in much of the world!

Although growth per capita began to increase very slowly after 1300, the world economy didn't really begin to take off until the Industrial Revolution in 1750. This is when machinery powered by steam engines began to replace human and animal power.

Under the spur of industry, first England, and then other countries, such as the United States, France, and Germany, finally began to experience sustained long-term economic growth and rising standards of living. In this way the industrial revolution marked a key turning point in human history. Before the Industrial Revolution, economic growth was slow and halting. After the Industrial Revolution, economic growth became rapid and sustained.

*   *   *

From our analysis of these Ten Levers of Growth, we now know that economic growth is a complex process that is driven by a diversity of factors. Accordingly, no single "magic policy bullet" can be fired to get America back on a path toward robust and sustainable long-term growth. Rather, any policy blueprint to promote long-term, sustainable economic growth must attack the process on all available fronts—free markets, free trade, the fostering of entrepreneurship, higher savings and investment, reduced oil import dependency, a sound health care system, and so on.

The remaining chapters use our Ten Levers of Growth in conjunction with the GDP Growth Driver equation to critique each of the major policy initiatives of the Obama administration—and to illustrate why so many of them have gone wrong. As part of this critique, we will also offer the set of policy alternatives featured in our Seeds of Prosperity blueprint. As you will see, if America is to resume its journey along the path of long-term prosperity, we need a complete overhaul of virtually every key policy area—from fiscal, monetary, and tax policy to energy, health care, and trade reform.

Why Adam Smith Beat Nikita Khrushchev

The collapse of the Soviet Union offers a compelling validation of Adam Smith's free-market capitalism and the Solow growth model while highlighting the importance of Schumpeterian entrepreneurship. In 1960, Nikita Khrushchev, premier of the Soviet Union, addressed the United Nations in New York City. He declared to the United States and the other democracies, "We will bury you. Your grandchildren will live under communism."

Many economists at the time took Khrushchev's threats seriously. They were particularly alarmed to see capital investment in new plants and equipment grow rapidly in the Soviet Union from the 1950s through the 1980s. At first, this capital investment produced very rapid increases in economic growth. These increases were so rapid that some economists in the United States mistakenly predicted the Soviet Union would someday surpass the United States economically.

However, just as the Solow growth model predicts, the gains to growth from this capital investment began to rapidly diminish for the Soviet Union. The problem lay in the Achilles' heel of the Soviets' centrally planned economy—a failure to discover and implement new technologies.

This lack of technological change is a problem common to all centrally planned economies. In centrally planned economies, the executives in charge of running the businesses are government employees, not entrepreneurs. Their pay depends merely on producing the quantity of output specified in the government's economic plan rather than, like entrepreneurs, discovering new, better, and lower-cost ways to produce goods. The result for the Soviet Union would eventually be Solow's stagnant growth trap—and the Communist empire collapsed.

Ultimately, what the Soviet central planners failed to understand is that economic growth depends more on technological change than on increases in capital per hour and that the innovation necessary for rapid technological change cannot take place in an entrepreneurial vacuum.

Endnotes

1. Richard K. Lester, Andrew Bernard, Frank Levy, and Micky Tripathi, "Manufacturing in Massachusetts: Why Does it Matter? How Have We Done? Where Do We Stand?" Discussed in "Why manufacturing matters; Study released by Raytheon," *Business Wire* (September 22, 1995), http://www.allbusiness.com/labor-employment/labor-sector-performance-labor-force/7163005-1.html.

PART II

Fixing America's Destructive Duo: Monetary and Fiscal Policy

What role did the Federal Reserve play in creating the housing bubble that led to the 2007–2009 financial crisis? What kind of leadership do we need at the Federal Reserve to ensure long-term growth? And can we really fiscally stimulate our way out of a decade of economic stagnation and zero wage growth? The next two chapters address these critical questions.

The monetary policy analysis in Chapter 3, "Why an Easy-Money Street Is a Dead End," makes it abundantly clear that the Federal Reserve, under the leadership of first Alan Greenspan and then Ben Bernanke, did indeed play a key role in inflating the housing bubble by keeping interest rates artificially low for far too long. Our analysis also shows that the much bigger problem with the Federal Reserve now is an almost total abandonment of the type of "rules-based" leadership epitomized by chairmen such as Paul Volcker, who fiercely protected the Fed's independence. Critical to our GDP Growth Drivers analysis, we also show that the Fed has played a key role in exacerbating all four major structural imbalances in our economy with its often ultra-easy money policies and excessive attempts at discretionary "fine-tuning."

Chapter 4, "Why You Can't Stimulate Your Way to Prosperity," critiques our current fiscal policy, making it abundantly clear that America cannot tax and spend and fiscally stimulate its way to long-term prosperity. Rather than creating sufficient jobs to drive down the unemployment rate and boost wage levels, the Obama fiscal stimulus has been far more effective at creating a massive public debt that will choke economic growth down the road. The best lesson from this analysis is that we must wean ourselves from the idea that we can stimulate our way to prosperity. Instead, we must embrace the principle that only through reforms that address our economy's major structural imbalances can we return to the road of long-term prosperity.

chapter three

Why an Easy-Money Street Is a Dead End

> *"There ain't no right way to do the wrong thing."*
>
> Country singer Toby Keith

When it comes to sowing the seeds of America's economic stagnation, even the mighty U.S. Federal Reserve cannot avoid blame. Indeed, the Fed's activism over the past decade has played a key role in creating the large, growth-killing structural imbalances in our GDP Growth Driver equation. With its extended walk down Easy-Money Street, the Fed has simultaneously overstimulated consumption, depressed business investment, accommodated excessive growth in government expenditures, and reinforced chronic trade imbalances.

Historically, the United States has had two types of Fed chairmen, embracing very different philosophies about the proper role of the Fed in managing the economy and overseeing the financial system. One type has been embodied by chairmen such as Paul Volcker and William McChesney Martin, Jr. These Fed chairmen have fiercely protected the Fed's independence and put the goals of price stability and a sound currency ahead of political expediency and growth at any cost.

For example, during the 1960s, William McChesney Martin established the principle that an independent Federal Reserve need not accommodate the profligate deficit spending of the White House and Congress. This concept of "Fed accommodation" of budget deficits is particularly important in our narrative, so it is worth at least a brief explanation in case you're unfamiliar with the concept.

One way to finance the budget deficit is for the U.S. Treasury Department to sell bonds to the general public. One problem with this type of bond financing is that it may drive up interest rates. As the economy rebounds, the Treasury Department has to offer higher interest rates to attract enough investors to buy its bonds.

From the perspective of the GDP Growth Driver equation, the obvious problem with this type of bond financing is that as interest rates rise, business investment falls, along with demand for "big ticket" consumer durables such as homes and autos. This phenomenon is known as "crowding out," and it is one of the principal problems of using a deficit-financed fiscal stimulus to boost growth. To put the crowding-out problem most simply, any increase in government expenditures to stimulate the economy may be offset in whole or in part by a corresponding decrease in business investment and consumption because of the effects of higher interest rates.

A second way to finance the budget deficit is through Fed accommodation of the U.S. Treasury Department's bond sales. In this accommodation scenario, the U.S. Treasury Department bypasses the public bond market and sells its bonds *directly* to the Federal Reserve.

As we explained in Chapter 1, "America's Four Growth Drivers Stall and Our Economy Stagnates," a big problem with such Fed accommodation is that it can be inflationary. This linkage arises because when the Fed buys the U.S. Treasury bonds, it is effectively printing money to do so.

The second problem with Fed accommodation is even more important within the context of this chapter. This problem is that Fed accommodation enables the White House and Congress to engage in fiscally irresponsible behavior that leads to ever-larger deficits and similar and significant inflationary problems down the road.

This problem of fiscally irresponsible behavior is precisely the one that Federal Reserve Chairman William McChesney Martin, Jr. had with President Lyndon Johnson during the 1960s. Johnson wanted to simultaneously prosecute the Vietnam War and pass his social welfare Great Society programs, while running large budget deficits. To Martin, President Johnson's refusal to choose between "guns and butter" was a recipe for an explosive bout of inflation and a destabilization of America's longer-term economic growth path. For this reason, and to the extreme anger of President Johnson, Martin refused to accommodate the Treasury Department's additional borrowing.

In 1979, in the midst of one of America's darkest inflationary episodes, Paul Volcker, appointed Fed chairman by President Jimmy Carter, likewise drew a line in the sand on behalf of price stability and sound money. Following a "monetarist" formula pioneered by economist Milton Friedman, the Volcker Fed allowed interest rates to rise dramatically and thereby broke the back of a dangerous stagflationary cycle that had plagued almost the entire 1970s. In a classic case of "no pain, no gain," Volcker's tough interest rate love helped set the stage for a 1980s boom. Indeed, the subsequent fall in inflation was like a large tax cut for investment. It is not an understatement to give the disinflation of the 1980s—and the Volcker Fed's implicit tax cut—a starring role in the revival of an American prosperity that lasted right up to 2000.

The Return of Fed Activism

Fed chairmen such as William McChesney Martin and Paul Volcker have fiercely protected the independence of the Federal Reserve and conducted Fed policy with price stability and sound money foremost in their minds. But the United States has also experienced another type of Fed chairman. This type is an activist who strongly believes that monetary policy should be used in a discretionary manner not just to keep the American economy on its basic track but also to fine-tune the economy over the ups and downs of the business cycle. This type of Fed chairman has been embodied in the two men who have presided over the Fed since the beginning of America's economic stagnation in 2000—Alan Greenspan and Ben Bernanke.

Both Greenspan and Bernanke deserve credit for portions of their stewardship of the Fed—Greenspan for guiding the Fed to allow the economy to grow more rapidly in response to the productivity boom of the mid-1990s, and Bernanke for bold policy to counteract the 2007–2009 financial crisis. But both Fed leaders have significantly contributed to an unwelcome return of Fed activism in managing the economy.

In theory, activist monetary policy has great appeal as a discretionary policy tool. According to many textbook models, as soon as a recession threatens, the Federal Reserve can simply cut interest rates and thereby stimulate both business investment and consumer spending on big-ticket items such as autos and housing. In textbooks, at least, the economy always recovers.

Although this all seems simple, the history of the application of discretionary monetary policy teaches us a very different lesson. In practice, the fog of economic fluctuations has often led activist Fed chairmen to some very bad mistakes. A classic case in point is the tenure of Alan Greenspan.

The Maestro or a Bubble Maker?

The popular mythology of Mr. Greenspan portrays him as "the Maestro" of finance. In some respects, this reputation is well deserved. For example, Greenspan deserves kudos for his keen understanding of the 1990s productivity boom as well as his deft handling of both the 1987 stock market crash and the effects of the 1997–1998 Asian financial crisis.

These triumphs notwithstanding, history also teaches us that Mr. Greenspan was an architect of two asset bubbles and two of the worst stock market collapses that followed in the wake of those bubbles bursting. Consider first the growth and then the bursting of the tech bubble and the stock market crash that followed.

During the development of the stock market tech bubble of the late 1990s, the Fed raised interest rates far too slowly. The Fed then burst that tech bubble with a series of dramatic interest rate hikes beginning in June 1999 and ending with a 50 basis point bang in May 2000—fully two months *after* the stock market had begun its descent. These interest rate hikes not only helped push the economy into the March 2001 recession, but they also helped shave off more than 60% of the technology-laden NASDAQ's value by the time the March 2001 recession began.

The stock market bubble had barely burst when the Fed began constructing another bubble—the housing bubble. In the wake of the September 11, 2001 terrorist attacks, Greenspan slashed interest rates to 1% and kept them artificially low for years. These artificially low interest rates helped inflate the housing bubble as rapidly rising home prices allowed American homeowners to go on a mortgage refinancing spree that effectively turned their homes into ATMs. As home values rose, Americans could take more and more equity out of their homes and use that cash to fuel their consumption needs. Of course, this stimulus to consumption cushioned the blow of the 2001 recession and continued to boost economic activity—for a while.

During this time, the current Fed chairman, Ben Bernanke, was also a key player in the Fed's role in the housing bubble. As a member of the Board of Governors of the Federal Reserve System from 2002 to 2005, Bernanke supported the Fed's easy-money policies. When Bernanke moved to the White House in June 2005, he continued his accommodative stance of the Fed until he was sworn in as Fed chairman on February 1, 2006.

It was during this era of easy money that growth-killing structural imbalances in America's GDP Growth Driver equation would become more and more pronounced. Consumption rose from its historical average of about 65% of the GDP Growth Driver equation to as high as 70%. This overconsumption was reflected in a historically low savings rate that translated into inadequate business investment. In this way, the Fed's easy money struck a blow against the job-creation capabilities of the American economy.

President Obama Crosses the Activist Rubicon

"Probably the commonest way economists measure the stance of monetary policy is the Taylor rule, named after John Taylor, the Stanford University economist who invented it. The rule is a guide to what interest rates should be, depending on the amount of slack in the economy and the inflation rate.

"It says that if there is no output gap (that is, if GDP is in line with the economy's capacity) and inflation is equal to the central bank's target, then interest rates should be at a neutral level, causing the economy neither to accelerate nor to slow down. If an output gap opens up, so that GDP outstrips long run capacity, or

inflation rises above target, rates should be above neutral. If there is slack in the economy or inflation dips, policy should be eased."

Economist (October 2007)[1]

Even though President Barack Obama inherited the legacy of an activist Fed chairman, he also took full ownership of the Fed's legacy once he reappointed Bernanke to a second term in January 2010. It is important to note that the housing bubble never would have grown so large and never would have caused so much damage if the Fed had simply followed a monetary rule such as the "Taylor rule," set forth by Stanford economist and monetarist John Taylor and described in the preceding excerpt from *The Economist*.

In a nutshell, the Taylor rule guides the Federal Reserve to raise interest rates when inflation rises above a certain target and guides the Fed to cut interest rates when the economy falls a certain level below its potential growth rate. Essentially, the Taylor rule promotes a simple guide to the conduct of monetary policy. Exhibit 3.1 illustrates the significant divergence between the Bernanke Fed's actual easy-money interest rate policy and that which would have been dictated by adhering to the Taylor rule.

Historically, Nobel Laureate Milton Friedman believed that such monetary rules would triumph over discretionary activism in terms of bringing about long-term American economic prosperity. He believed this for at least two reasons.

First, a rules-based approach would prevent the Federal Reserve from becoming a tool of the political system. In the absence of rules, a Federal Reserve chairman beholden to a president or political party may seek to engineer an accelerated economic expansion before a major election. A classic example is Fed Chairman Arthur Burns, who many economists believe did just that for Richard Nixon in 1972.

Even though Nixon won re-election that year, the inevitable result of the Burns easy-money era was a spike in inflation followed by a recession during the difficult stagflationary years that would soon follow.

Exhibit 3.1   The Fed Diverges Sharply from the Taylor Rule

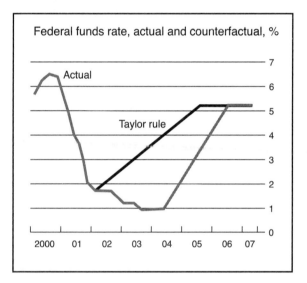

Source: John Taylor, "Housing and Monetary Policy," September 2007.

The second reason why Friedman believed that the Federal Reserve should not engage in an activist discretionary policy relates to the concept of the fog of economic fluctuations. This fog of uncertainty often turns the Federal Reserve into a "bad driver." It has a dangerous tendency to stomp on the accelerator to stimulate an economy that might be slowing down and then stomp on the brakes as the economy might be overheating. The result of such a "bad driver Fed" is to accentuate cyclical fluctuations rather than moderate them. Friedman believed that only by having certainty and rules about the expansion of the money supply could such fluctuations be avoided.

Despite their successes in some important areas, our last two Federal Reserve chairmen, Greenspan and Bernanke, have taught us that there is much truth in what Friedman said about the dangers of discretionary activism. In fact, Bernanke appears to be taking Fed discretionary policies to an entirely new level of activism that is causing structural imbalances in both the net export and government spending drivers in the GDP Growth Driver equation.

The Road to American Prosperity Cannot Be Paved with a Cheap Dollar

In its traditional role, an activist Fed lowers interest rates to stimulate business investment and the purchase of interest-rate-sensitive big-ticket consumer items such as autos and housing. In this way, Fed interest rate cuts represent a domestic strategy for stimulating GDP growth.

During much of the 2000s, the Fed has often also implicitly sought to stimulate GDP growth by stimulating export demand through a falling dollar. To understand why this strategy has pitfalls internationally (for example, in European economies), it is essential to understand the following:

Lower interest rates from the Federal Reserve put downward pressure on the dollar relative to other currencies such as the euro. The reason is that as American interest rates fall relative to the rest of the world, foreign investors are less likely to invest in U.S. bonds. These investors, therefore, have less need to exchange their currencies for dollars, and a reduction in demand for the dollar results in a fall in the dollar's exchange rate.

In this way, the Fed's monetary policy is one factor explaining the dollar's significant decline in value relative to the euro that occurred between 2001 and 2008. Of course, the dollar's fall relative to the euro helps boost American exports to Europe and U.S. GDP growth, while European exports to the U.S. suffer. In this way, the weak dollar contributed to sluggish European growth. To be clear here, over the past several years, the dollar has also experienced several cyclical uptrends—most notably during the midst of the 2007–2009 financial crisis and during the European contagion of 2010. During both of these volatile periods, investors around the world flocked to the safety of the dollar which rose relative to currencies like the euro. However, despite these short-term upswings, the dollar's value is likely in a longer-term decline because of a combination of soaring budget deficits and inflationary pressures from the Federal Reserve's very accommodative monetary policy during and after the financial crisis.

If you were to apply a simple textbook analysis of the Fed's strategy to stimulate export-driven growth, it should work. That is, a weaker dollar should make American exports more attractive to the rest of the world while suppressing the purchase of imports. In this way, the chronic U.S. trade deficit should come back into balance, and net exports should go toward zero to the benefit of GDP growth.

This textbook adjustment process has not, however, significantly reduced chronic U.S. trade imbalances with America's largest trading partner, China, or with the rest of the world. The reasons have to do with three extenuating circumstances: China pegs its currency primarily to the U.S. dollar; many of the world's commodities, including oil, are priced in dollars; and a "dollar carry trade" emerged in response to the Fed's low interest rate policy.

With respect the first circumstance, China's government pegs the value of its currency, the yuan, to a basket of currencies that is heavily weighted to the dollar. In effect, this is a de facto "hard dollar peg" at a fixed exchange rate. This peg means that no matter how low the dollar falls, the yuan falls in lockstep with it. As a consequence, the U.S. trade deficit with China is difficult to reduce, because needed exchange rate adjustments are neutralized by China's dollar peg. (Meanwhile, within China, the undervalued yuan attracts "hot money" flows into the country. This attraction has led to significant inflation and speculative bubbles in both the stock and real estate markets.)

A second reason why a weak dollar strategy has not significantly reduced chronic trade imbalances—or spurred significant economic growth—has to do with the fact that oil, as well as many other internationally traded commodities ranging from cocoa, coffee, and corn to gold, soybeans, and wheat, are priced in U.S. dollars in world markets. As numerous studies of the correlation between the value of the dollar and commodity prices have shown, this linkage means that every time the Fed cuts interest rates and the value of the U.S. dollar falls, Americans wind up paying more for their oil and gasoline and other commodity needs. This, in turn, means that even as the United States sells more exports because of a cheaper dollar, it has to pay more for its imported oil and other commodities. Therefore, any benefits of a weak dollar in reducing the trade balance are greatly diminished.

More broadly, Stanford economist John Taylor has persuasively argued that the Fed's artificially low interest rates didn't just help spawn the housing bubble. They also helped drive the economy deeper into recession and then prolonged the crisis by sharply driving up oil and other commodities prices.

In this regard, when the financial crisis began in August 2007, the Bernanke Fed cut the Fed funds rate from 5.25% to 2.0% by April 2008. In this case, the Taylor rule would likewise have called for a rate cut—but one not nearly as sharp. Taylor wrote about this overreaction by the Bernanke Fed and its impact on oil prices and the economy:

> "When the federal funds rate was cut, oil prices broke out of the $60–$70 per barrel range and then rose rapidly throughout the first year of the financial crisis. Clearly, this bout of high oil prices hit the economy hard as gasoline prices

skyrocketed and automobile sales plummeted in the spring and summer of 2008...[T]his interest-rate cut helped raise oil and other commodity prices and thereby prolonged the crisis."[2]

The third reason why the Fed's weak dollar strategy hasn't addressed America's chronic trade imbalance has to do with a pernicious "dollar carry trade" that the Fed's accommodative policies have spawned. In this dollar carry trade, speculators borrow money in U.S. dollars at the artificially low interest rates set by the Fed and then invest those dollars overseas in higher-yielding assets such as emerging markets and energy and commodities.

This carry trade simultaneously drives down the value of the dollar even as it helps create a speculative bubble in these other higher-yielding assets. In the process, the low interest rates and easy money do little to stimulate domestic business investment—the real key to reigniting the American economy and taking us down the path of long-term prosperity. Indeed, present policy may actually discourage risky lending to American small businesses.

Where Have You Gone, William McChesney Martin?

A final problem with the discretionary activism of the current Federal Reserve is the growth-stalling matter of the Fed's ongoing accommodation of the federal budget deficit through its large-scale purchase of U.S. Treasury securities. Indeed, unlike Fed Chairman William McChesney Martin, Jr., who stood up to President Johnson in the 1960s, the present Fed has drawn no such line in the sand on behalf of fiscal restraint. Instead, through a dramatic expansion of its balance sheet, the Fed has enabled a rapid run-up in the percentage of growth accounted for by government expenditures in the GDP Growth Driver equation—and no good long-term growth can come from that.

*   *   *

In closing this chapter, we note that asset bubbles and the economic consequences of the 2007–2009 financial crisis have led to calls for changes both in the financial system in general and in the Federal Reserve's powers in particular. The vanishing of $10 trillion of household wealth has made many people justifiably angry.

It is hard to avoid assigning some of the blame to the Fed's accommodative monetary policy that exacerbated mispricing of risk and asset bubbles. But reforms should improve the Fed's performance, not trim its sails. The Fed needs to remain independent and manage the nation's monetary policy and be the lender of last resort, as it has in the past.

That said, the almost unlimited powers of lending that the Fed has exercised in both creating credit and assisting particular financial institutions in the past three years must be curbed. We will discuss this issue in more detail in Chapter 10, "How to Prevent Another Financial Crisis—and Housing Bubble." For now we will say that such authority should be both restricted in duration and subject to approval by the U.S. Treasury Department and elected officials.

Most importantly, the Fed should turn its emphasis away from discretionary fine-tuning and toward pursuing policies that are in the interests of sound, long-term growth. The Fed has made some significant errors in its almost-100-year history. It has bounced back from past errors and added to the economy's vitality in key periods.

What we need now at the Federal Reserve is leadership in the tradition of William McChesney Martin, Jr. and Paul Volcker. We need leaders who will fiercely guard the Fed's independence while following a rules-based policy aimed at ensuring price stability and sound money. To borrow from the lyrics of country singer Toby Keith cited at the beginning of this chapter, when it comes to discretionary activism at the Fed, "There ain't no right way to do the wrong thing."

Endnotes

1. "Fast and Loose." *The Economist*. October 18, 2007.

2. John B. Taylor. *Getting Off Track*. Stanford, California: Hoover Institution Press, 2009.

chapter four

Why You Can't Stimulate Your Way to Prosperity

"Throughout 2008, Larry Summers, the Harvard economist, built the case for a big but surgical stimulus package. [However,] the stimulus approach that has emerged on Capitol Hill abandoned the Summers parameters.

"In a fateful decision, Democratic leaders merged the temporary stimulus measure with their permanent domestic agenda.... It's easy to see why Democrats decided to do this. They could rush through permanent policies they believe in. Plus, they could pay for them with borrowed money. ... But they've created a sprawling, undisciplined smorgasbord, which has spun off a series of unintended consequences."

David Brooks, *New York Times* (January 2009)[1]

Upon his inauguration on January 20, 2009, President Barack Obama unquestionably inherited a very difficult economic situation from former President George W. Bush. The U.S. recession was in its thirteenth month, the unemployment rate had climbed to a 16-year high of 7.2%, over 11 million Americans were jobless,[2] and economic recovery was nowhere visible on the horizon.

Despite the seriousness of the situation, one of President Obama's first acts was to turn over responsibility for the design of the stimulus bill—eventually dubbed the American Recovery and Reinvestment Act of 2009—to the congressional leadership of Senate Majority

Leader Harry Reid (D-NV) and Speaker of the House Nancy Pelosi (D-CA).

This abdication of design (or, to be more old-fashioned, leadership) would turn out to be a stumble for the new president. Together, the congressional leadership would prove to be far more adept at crafting a "sprawling, undisciplined smorgasbord" of pork barrel legislation than a stimulus package likely to help spur economic recovery, job creation, and longer-term growth.

From the perspective of our GDP Growth Drivers analysis, the Obama smorgasbord will, over the next decade, only further exacerbate that part of the glaring structural imbalance in the economy caused by too much government spending. In part because of the stimulus, the cumulative budget deficit will double from $4.4 to $9.3 trillion. Moreover, by 2019, the debt held by the public will have soared from 57% of GDP in 2009 to 82%, a figure not seen since World War II.[3]

President Obama's transfer of leadership on the stimulus package to the Congress was inexplicable, inexcusable, and ironic. The approach was inexplicable because the new president was at the height of his popularity and power. He had just won a near-landslide victory, and his long coattails had given him a solidly Democratic Congress. If there were any time he could have any stimulus bill he wanted, January 2009 was it.

President Obama's leadership vacuum on the stimulus was likewise both inexcusable and ironic because he had top talent at his fingertips to do any fiscal stimulus properly. His experts included White House advisor Larry Summers and his handpicked director at the Office of Management and Budget, Peter Orszag.

Prior to the president's election, Summers had distilled three of the most important conditions for an effective fiscal stimulus into a memorable sound bite: Any stimulus must be "timely, targeted, and temporary."

- A fiscal stimulus must be timely because if the effects of the stimulus arrive *after* a recovery is under way, the stimulus may simply exacerbate inflation, force the Federal Reserve to raise interest rates, and thereby choke off the recovery.

- Any fiscal stimulus also should be precisely targeted at the consumers, businesses, and government entities that are most likely to spend the stimulus quickly and fully. Such targeting minimizes the cost of the stimulus while helping ensure timeliness.

- Finally, any fiscal stimulus should be temporary because fiscal stimulus packages typically are financed through budget deficits. Permanent fiscal stimuli exacerbate budget deficits so that over time, higher interest payments on the debt create "fiscal drag," higher interest rates crowd out business investment and consumer spending on autos and housing, and the economy slows back down.

Orszag clearly concurred with this "Summers test." Almost exactly one year before Obama was sworn into office, Orszag—then the Director of the CBO—warned Congress that "Poorly timed policies may do harm by aggravating inflationary pressures and needlessly increasing federal debt if they stimulate the economy after it has already started to recover."[4]

Orszag likewise gave this damning indictment of precisely the kinds of large-scale public-works projects the 2009 Obama stimulus bill would be littered with:

> "Conceptually, spending on these kinds of projects seems to offer an appealing way to counteract an economic downturn. ... Practically speaking, however, public works involve long start-up lags. Large-scale construction projects of any type

require years of planning and preparation. Even those that are 'on the shelf' generally cannot be undertaken quickly enough to provide timely stimulus to the economy. ... In general, many if not most of these projects could end up making the economic situation worse because they would stimulate the economy at the time that expansion was already well under way."[5]

The U.S. economy would wind up paying a very heavy price for the lack of White House leadership on the stimulus package. Because of its poor design and its repeated violations of the "temporary, timely, and targeted" tests, the 2009 smorgasbord would do little to stop the unemployment rate from soaring close to the double digits—even as it contributed heavily to a ballooning budget deficit.

To understand just why the 2009 fiscal stimulus went so wrong—and, more importantly, to understand why we cannot "stimulate" our way back to economic prosperity—it's useful to review some of the history and logic behind the idea of fiscal stimulus. After we do that, we can discuss some of the "do's and don'ts" of an effective fiscal stimulus and then measure the Obama stimulus by this "do's and don'ts" yardstick.

From John Maynard Keynes to the Kennedy Tax Cut Revolution

The concept of using a fiscal stimulus to heal an economy from recession dates back to the Great Depression and the writings of the celebrated Depression-era economist John Maynard Keynes. The GDP Growth Drivers equation introduced in Chapter 1, "America's Four Growth Drivers Stall and Our Economy Stagnates," helps us understand the seductive lure of traditional Keynesian fiscal stimulus.

Recall from Chapter 1 that GDP growth is driven by only four components. If consumption, investment, and net exports are all performing poorly, it follows that the government must step in and increase government spending to make up the difference— or so goes the Keynesian "government as spender of last resort" argument.

The problem with this Keynesian argument is that it fails to take into account the dynamic, longer-term impacts of budget deficits on interest rates, inflation, exchange rates, and the levels of consumption, investment, and net exports. It is also well worth noting that in this world, it matters little how the government spends funds or even whether a massive budget deficit results. Just dig a ditch and fill it up and you've created a job and wage income, and that person will start consuming again to stimulate the economy.

To this day, a spirited debate continues among economists about whether Keynesian spending, a loosening of monetary policy, or some combination thereof got America out of the Great Depression. There is little disagreement, however, that almost 30 years after Keynes and FDR's "New Deal," Democratic President John F. Kennedy turned Keynesianism on its head. JFK did so by advocating tax cuts on investment rather than increased government expenditures as a more effective form of fiscal stimulus.

The central idea behind Kennedy's theme was that tax cuts would more directly spur an increase in business investment in the GDP Growth Drivers equation than increased government spending. In 1961, in a special message to Congress on taxation, President Kennedy had this to say about the critical role of business investment in the GDP Growth Drivers equation in fighting slow growth and trade deficits in an era of increased global competition:

> "The history of our economy has been one of rising productivity, based on improvement in skills, advances in technology, and a growing supply of more efficient tools and equipment. This rise

has been reflected in rising wages and standards of living for our workers, as well as a healthy rate of growth for the economy as a whole. It has also been the foundation of our leadership in world markets, even as we enjoyed the highest wage rates in the world.

"Today, as we face serious pressure on our balance of payments position, we must give special attention to the modernization of our plant and equipment. Forced to reconstruct after wartime devastation, our friends abroad now possess a modern industrial system helping to make them formidable competitors in world markets. If our own goods are to compete with foreign goods in price and quality, both at home and abroad, we shall need the most efficient plant and equipment."

Since Kennedy's time, every time a recession has occurred, there has been a great battle over whether to increase government spending or tax cuts for stimulus. Democrats typically favor increased government spending, and Republicans typically prefer tax cuts.

In fact, economic researchers have had a lot to say about the virtues of government expenditures versus tax cuts as countercyclical, recession-fighting tools. More broadly, they have had a lot to say about how to implement an appropriate fiscal stimulus. From this research, we can compile a list of "do's and don'ts" that help us illustrate that, in most cases, the 2009 fiscal stimulus got it exactly wrong. The first eight of these "do's and don'ts" provide a critique of the stimulus package. The remaining three call into question the need for any stimulus beyond some very targeted and temporary government transfer programs to help those most afflicted by the recession.

#1: Do prefer tax cuts to government expenditure programs

This first "do" follows from some of the latest economic research. In a study conducted for the National Bureau of Economic Research,

Harvard economists Alberto Alesina and Silvia Ardagna analyzed fiscal stimuli in 21 Organization for Economic Cooperation and Development (OECD) countries, from Australia, Austria, and Canada to the Netherlands, Norway, Sweden, and the United Kingdom.[6] The study identified 91 different attempts at fiscal stimulus since 1970 in these 21 countries. The results: The most successful fiscal stimulus programs depended almost entirely on cuts in business and income taxes. In contrast, relying on increased government expenditures most often resulted in much less growth.

In addition, recent research by Christina Romer (currently chair of the Council of Economic Advisers) and David Romer provides evidence that tax changes more generally have a large and persistent "multiplier effect." For example, they found that a tax hike equivalent to 1% of U.S. GDP reduces output just over 1% within a year, but the magnitude amplifies in the following periods to reach an effect of nearly 3% after three years.[7]

Despite the apparent advantage of tax cuts in providing stimulus power, the 2009 stimulus was heavily skewed toward government expenditures. Indeed, tax cuts constituted only a third of the stimulus package. This heavy government expenditure skew has only worsened the structural imbalance in the GDP Growth Drivers equation while slowing future long-term growth.

#2: Don't rely on government expenditure programs with long spend-outs

One of the biggest reasons why the Obama stimulus failed to prevent the unemployment rate from rising to double digits in the first year of the package—in contrast to the administration's forecast—was that less than a third of the funds found their way into the national economy. A large part of the problem was construction projects with slow spend-outs. The CBO had warned about this problem as the stimulus package was being debated.

According to the CBO, less than $5 billion of the $30 billion set aside for highway spending would be spent by the end of 2010. Just one in seven dollars spent on green energy programs would be injected into the economy by the middle of 2010. Less than $1 billion of the $6 billion plan to expand broadband access would be spent by 2011. And only $26 billion out of $274 billion in infrastructure spending would be delivered by the end of the first year of the stimulus.[8]

Federal Reserve Chairman Ben Bernanke likewise warned Congress about the lack of timeliness before the 2009 stimulus bill passed:

> "To be useful, a fiscal stimulus package should be implemented quickly and structured so that its effects on aggregate spending are felt as much as possible within the next twelve months or so. Stimulus that comes too late will not help support economic activity in the near term, and it could be actively destabilizing if it comes at a time when growth is already improving. Thus, fiscal measures that involve long lead times or result in additional economic activity only over a protracted period, whatever their intrinsic merits might be, will not provide stimulus when it is most needed."[9]

Despite the clarity of Chairman Bernanke's warning, it fell on deaf ears.

#3: Don't try to disguise permanent government expenditure programs as temporary fiscal stimulus

One major reason why the Obama stimulus was too heavily skewed toward government spending is that the Democrats used their majorities in both houses of Congress to pass pet projects and programs that were only tangentially related to the stimulus. As David Brooks noted about the "smorgasbord stimulus," these included big spending increases for items such as alternative energy subsidies and entitlement spending.

In fact, President Obama set a dangerous precedent by trumpeting projects such as a green energy initiative in the stimulus. Although such an initiative may be part of a broader energy policy, trying to create such an industry under the guise of a fiscal stimulus represents a gross violation of the "Summers test" of temporariness. As Obama's own budget director, Peter Orszag, would chide: "Some of the candidates for public works, such as grant-funded initiatives to develop alternative energy sources, are totally impractical for countercyclical policy, regardless of whatever other merits they may have."[10]

Moreover, boosting entitlement programs as part of the stimulus package was as absurd as it was irresponsible. As we discuss in Chapter 8, "Cutting the Gordian Knot of Entitlements," a major problem facing the American economy is its out-of-control entitlements programs.

#4: Do favor permanent tax cuts over temporary ones

Democrats and orthodox Keynesian economists like to argue that if you have to impose a tax cut to stimulate the economy, it better be temporary. Otherwise, the resulting permanent tax cut will add to the federal budget deficit and therefore will be self-defeating.

This argument is inconsistent with both economic theory and considerable research. As Stanford economist John Taylor has observed, "temporary increases in income will *not* lead to significant increases in consumption. However, if increases are longer-term, as in the case of a permanent tax cut, then consumption is increased, and by a significant amount."[11]

Unfortunately, most of the tax relief offered in the Obama stimulus for both businesses and individuals was temporary. In contrast, a permanent cut in the corporate income tax—a long overdue structural reform—would boost both investment and workers' wages. A cut in the payroll tax for lower- and middle-income workers would similarly boost consumer spending.

Regrettably, in his 2010 budget submission, the president moved in exactly the opposite direction by calling for tax *increases* on business investment and capital formation to fund escalations in government spending.

#5: Do focus primarily on stimulating business investment if the goal is both short-term stimulus and longer-term growth

One of the worst flaws of the 2009 stimulus is that it failed to address one of the most glaring structural weaknesses in America's GDP Growth Drivers equation—underinvestment by the business sector. As we saw in Chapter 2, "How to Lift the American Economy with the Ten Levers of Growth," unless business investment is boosted, we will not have the production capacity and increased rates of technological innovation and productivity needed to ensure longer-term prosperity.

Despite the importance of business investment in America's economic recovery, it fared extremely poorly in the Obama fiscal stimulus. Indeed, less than 3% of the total stimulus was targeted at the GDP Growth Drivers equation with the most power to generate jobs. As noted earlier (and it is worth repeating), once 2010 rolled around, President Obama called for tax *increases* on businesses.

#6: Do favor federal government transfer programs to meet the tests of timeliness and proper targeting

One of the few things that the Obama stimulus package did correctly was to increase expenditures for jobless benefits, such as extending unemployment compensation and boosting the food stamp program. These types of government transfer programs represent one of the fastest ways to get a stimulus into the economy by bolstering consumption.

#7: Do provide cash-strapped state governments with transfer payments that will help them finance their unemployment benefits programs and allow them to avoid contractionary cutbacks in spending and layoffs—but beware moral hazard

Unlike the federal government, state governments must balance their annual budgets. When a recession hits, tax revenues decline even as welfare payments increase. The resulting budget deficits force state governments either to raise taxes to cover the shortfall or to cut spending and lay off employees. In either case, the broader effect nationally is to deepen the recession, because either action—higher taxes or reduced spending and employment at the state level—is contractionary.

To avoid the contractionary ripple effects of state budget constraints, a fiscal stimulus can be more effective by increasing transfer payments to state governments so as to avoid tax hikes or layoffs. There are several important words of caution here, however.

First, some states may be in far better shape than others, depending on their resource endowments and the actions of their own public officials. For example, in any given recession, states that depend more on energy or agriculture may be better or worse off than states that are more dependent on manufacturing. By the same token, if a state's politicians are big spenders, that state can be far more vulnerable once recession hits.

Providing transfer payments to states that don't really need the money and that might otherwise use "rainy day funds" to ride out of recession doth not an effective stimulus make, either. By the same token, there's a strong element of "moral hazard" when the federal government starts bailing out states from their profligate spending ways.

With these caveats in mind, it may be said that including transfer payments to states was the second feature of the Obama stimulus package that appears to have been at least a mild success. Because of such transfer payments, state and local governments were able to maintain spending levels in 2009 at about the same levels as the previous year.

#8: Don't be Robin Hood or Huey Long in targeting a stimulus package

One of the biggest temptations during a recession, particularly one characterized by a budget crisis, is to seek to solve all problems like Robin Hood—by "taxing the rich." An equally compelling political temptation is engaging in Huey Long-style populist rhetoric in support of income redistribution under the guise of fiscal stimulus.

Often, these class warfare policies are cloaked in well crafted economic arguments. For example, Keynesian economists typically argue that it is better to target any fiscal stimulus to low-income people because such individuals will be more likely to spend, rather than save, their tax rebates or cuts.

This Robin Hood argument ignores that one of the broader goals of a fiscal stimulus is to temporarily increase consumption in the GDP equation. By leaving out the vast majority of consumers and only targeting the poor, you simply will not have enough stimulus power.

By the same token, "taxing the rich" during a recession to redistribute income to the poor is an appealing political message. However, it is unlikely to result in any net gain in GDP growth because of the negative effects of the tax on incentives, particularly for small business owners, who often are ensnared in the "tax the rich" net. And the amount of revenue raised from such taxes will not come close to ridding the economy of our long-term budget gap.

The Obama stimulus package featured neither Robin Hood nor Huey Long tax measures. However, the soaring budget deficits that have resulted in part from the stimulus package have led the Obama administration to subsequently engage in precisely the kind of class warfare rhetoric and "tax the rich" measures that are likely to be so counterproductive in restoring long-term growth to the American economy.

In light of the long-term structural weakness of the American economy, the most egregious tax increase sought by the president in his 2011 budget is a sharp increase in the capital gains tax. This is exactly the opposite direction from which the president should be moving, because any such tax hike will further depress business investment in the GDP Growth Drivers equation.

*   *   *

Our first eight "do's and don'ts" have provided a critique of the effectiveness—or lack thereof—of the 2009 stimulus package. The remaining "do's and don'ts" raise the broader question of whether any fiscal stimulus beyond fast-acting and highly targeted transfer payments was actually needed in 2009—and whether there might have been a better strategy to address the crisis.

#9: Don't use a fiscal stimulus to fix a recession triggered by a financial crisis

When country musician Toby Keith sang "There ain't no right way to do the wrong thing," he might well have been singing about the

Obama fiscal stimulus. Indeed, a strong argument can be made that even an appropriately designed fiscal stimulus of the magnitude proposed by the Obama administration was uncalled for in 2009. Unlike all previous recessions in the post-World War II period in America, the 2007–2009 crash was far more a financial crisis than a textbook recession.

In a typical postwar recession, aggregate demand falls off as either consumption or business investment flags. The simple Keynesian solution is to pump aggregate demand back up by boosting consumption and investment through tax cuts and/or by directly increasing government expenditures. If such a fiscal stimulus is properly designed and coordinated well with monetary policy, it has at least a decent chance of helping pull an economy back into recovery.

This "textbook recession" scenario was not, however, the situation facing the Obama administration in 2009 as it rushed to put into place a stimulus package. Although a falloff in consumption from a collapse of the housing bubble did indeed lead the United States into a recession in 2007, the much bigger problem by 2009 was the continued lack of availability of credit and liquidity for both households and businesses.

A policy solution aimed more precisely at recapitalizing the financial sector, more effectively reaching distressed homeowners with mortgage relief, providing increased investment incentives, and cutting the payroll tax would likely have been far more effective at lubricating the wheels of the economy than the poorly designed Obama fiscal stimulus.

#10: Do let automatic stabilizers do their jobs

In times of recession, the federal government doesn't necessarily have to pass a fiscal stimulus. The federal budget already has a built-in countercyclical fiscal stimulus in the form of "automatic stabilizers."

During a recession, government tax revenues fall both absolutely and relative to national income. The result is an effective lowering of both the personal income tax rate and corporate tax rates. In addition, even as tax liabilities are dropping, more people become eligible for government transfer programs such as unemployment compensation and food stamps.

According to some studies, these automatic stabilizer effects can be quite significant, offsetting close to 10% of any decline in GDP during a recession. Moreover, according to the Tax Policy Center, "additional stabilization from unemployment insurance, although smaller in total magnitude than that from the tax system, is estimated to be eight times as effective per dollar of lost revenue because more of the money is spent rather than saved."[12]

Again, it is no small irony that one of the experts who has offered one of the strongest arguments in support of automatic stabilizers is again President Obama's own budget director, Peter Orszag. In the aftermath of the 2001 recession, while a fellow at the Brookings Institution, Orszag wrote:

> "Unemployment insurance is a particularly effective stimulus. Not surprisingly, job loss is often associated with a decline in consumption, which then reduces demand for other goods and services as part of a negative cycle of increasing unemployment and declining economic activity.
>
> "The unemployment insurance program helps to break this negative cycle: By partially compensating for lost income, it lessens the reduction in spending that unemployment can cause. ... Recent academic research has shown that, dollar for dollar, the UI system is eight times as effective as the entire tax system in mitigating the impact of a recession."[13]

#11: Don't make a long-term structural economic problem worse by implementing a poorly crafted, short-term countercyclical fiscal stimulus

Rather than address America's longer-term structural imbalances, the Obama administration has continued to focus almost entirely on addressing short-run cyclical fluctuations. Not only is it doing so with little success, but it is all the while making our long-term structural problems much worse by running up huge budget deficits and raising taxes in a way that harms growth and job creation.

The longer-term impacts of fighting the wrong problem through soaring, poorly timed, and loosely targeted government expenditures are likely to be the crowding out of business investment because of higher interest rates and inflation associated with financing the deficit. That's one reason why, in its analysis of the Obama stimulus, the CBO concluded that the stimulus would actually slow the growth of the American economy over the longer term!

*   *   *

Given the rapidly growing debt and precarious fiscal shape of the United States, we have likely reached the point where the use of any further fiscal stimulus—as well designed as it may be—will be impractical for a very long time.

In the final analysis, the Obama fiscal stimulus has been far more effective at creating a massive public debt and all the attendant problems that come with it than at creating jobs and pulling the economy out of a recession. By doing so, not only has the Obama fiscal stimulus driven a stake through the heart of traditional Keynesian fiscal stimulus; it also has planted yet more seeds of America's economic stagnation over the longer term.

Indeed, in opting for a short-term fix rather than longer-term structural reforms, the Obama administration's fiscal policy is merely worsening America's structural problems. It is doing so directly by further ballooning the level of government expenditures in the GDP Growth Drivers equation and indirectly by suppressing critically needed business investment.

The best lesson we can learn from the failed Obama stimulus is that it's critical we reverse course. We need to wean ourselves from the idea that we can stimulate our way to prosperity. We need to embrace the principle that only through structural reforms will we return to the road of long-term prosperity.

As we will explain in subsequent chapters, such structural reform will mean saving more to benefit both domestic investment and future consumption. It will mean reforming entitlement programs so that we live within our means. These entitlement expenditures—and the deficits that come with them—will, over the longer term, limit our ability to defend our country, perform basic research, educate our children, and provide appropriate infrastructure for the broader economy.

Most importantly, structural reform of the American economy will mean tax reforms that will shift taxation toward consumption and lessen the tax bias against savings, investment, and job creation. Achieving such a shift will require a much greater awareness among both our politicians and the general public about the importance of business investment and the job- and wealth-creation processes.

Here, then, is our bottom line on the stimulus: Rather than expand government, we need to make government more effective and smaller, and shrink both the size of government and the size of our budget deficits and national debt. By doing so and by reducing Americans' tax burden, we will have a much better chance of stimulating consumption and investment in the GDP Growth Drivers equation, thereby promoting longer-term growth.

Endnotes

1. David Brooks. "Cleaner and Faster." *New York Times*. January 30, 2009.

2. These numbers reflect the December statistics. By the end of January 2009, the rate was 7.6%.

3. Congressional Budget Office. "A Preliminary Analysis of the President's Budget and an Update of CBO's Budget and Economic Outlook." March 2009.

4. CBO TESTIMONY. Statement of Peter R. Orszag, Director, Congressional Budget Office. "Options for Responding to Short-Term Economic Weakness." Before the Committee on Finance, United States Senate. January 22, 2008.

5. Ibid.

6. Alberto Alesina and Silvia Ardagna. "Large Changes in Fiscal Policy: Taxes Versus Spending." National Bureau of Economic Research. August 2009. Revised in October 2009.

7. Christina Romer and David H. Romer (forthcoming). "The Macroeconomic Effects of Tax Changes: Estimates Based on a New Measure of Fiscal Shocks." *American Economic Review*.

8. Congressional Budget Office. "A Preliminary Analysis of the President's Budget and an Update of CBO's Budget and Economic Outlook." March 2009.

9. Chairman Ben S. Bernanke. "The Economic Outlook." Testimony before the Committee on the Budget, U.S. House of Representatives. January 17, 2008.

10. CBO TESTIMONY, January 22, 2008.

11. John Taylor. "Why Permanent Tax Cuts Are the Best Stimulus: Short-Term Fiscal Policies Fail to Promote Long-Term Growth." *Wall Street Journal*, November 25, 2008. Taylor's argument follows directly from the permanent-income theory of Milton Friedman and the life-cycle theory of Franco Modigliani, which states that individuals will not

increase their expenditures unless their levels of income and wealth have permanently increased. This observation supports the use of permanent rather than temporary tax cuts. Any temporary tax cuts offered in times of economic turmoil are more likely to be saved rather than spent—and therefore don't provide any real stimulus.

12. "Economic Stimulus: How do automatic stabilizers work?" http://www. taxpolicycenter.org/briefing-book/background/stimulus/stabilizers.cfm.

13. Peter Orszag. "Unemployment Insurance as Economic Stimulus." Center on Budget and Policy Priorities. November 15, 2001.

PART III

Getting the "Big Three" Right: Tax, Trade, and Energy Policy

Why is American tax policy moving us in exactly the opposite direction of long-term economic prosperity? How important is trade reform in creating new jobs and laying the foundation for a sustainable economic recovery? Just how necessary is it to reduce America's high oil import dependence—and just how can that be done without harming American competitiveness? We answer these questions in the next three chapters as we examine three of the most important policy areas for the American economy.

The tax policy analysis in Chapter 5, "Why Raising Taxes Lowers America's Growth Rate," explains how raising taxes, particularly on business investment and capital income, is the best way to destroy jobs and innovation and ensure stagnant economic growth. Yet this is precisely the path that President Barack Obama's tax policy is traveling. This is truly a path to nowhere, because only through real tax reform can we overcome a rapidly increasing constraint on savings, investment, innovation, and growth.

The trade policy analysis in Chapter 6, "Why the Best 'Jobs Program' May Be Trade Reform," illustrates how large and chronic trade deficits have helped stall the American economy during the 2000s. Although the United States has rightly embraced free-trade principles, its major trading partners have systematically protected their own markets while engaging in a wide range of mercantilist "beggar thy neighbor" policies. These practices have destroyed millions of American jobs and helped hollow out our manufacturing base. Unless we engage in constructive trade reform, particularly with China, it will be virtually impossible to revitalize our manufacturing base and create enough new jobs to ensure long-term, sustainable growth.

The energy policy analysis in Chapter 7, "Why America's Foreign Oil Addiction Stunts Our Growth," underscores the critical importance of reducing America's oil import dependence not just from the perspective of geopolitical risk but, even more importantly, from the perspective of ensuring long-term economic growth. Presidents from Richard Nixon to Barack Obama have futilely tilted at the windmill of "energy independence." Although pursuing a policy of autarky is the wrong goal, we can significantly reduce our oil import dependence by harnessing market forces using flexible policies.

chapter five

Why Raising Taxes Lowers America's Growth Rate

"Not only is our tax system maddeningly complex, it penalizes work, discourages saving and investment, and hinders the competitiveness of American businesses."

President's Advisory Panel on Federal Tax Reform (2005)

Besides death and taxes, this too is certain: The American economy will never return to its maximum prosperity until it completes a very broad-based tax reform. This essential insight inexorably flows from our analyses of America's GDP Growth Driver equation and the Ten Levers of Growth.

As we have learned from those analyses, the American economy has entered a sustained period of slow GDP growth and zero income growth because of four significant structural imbalances that are stalling growth: overconsumption, underinvestment, excess government spending, and chronic trade deficits.

This chapter explains how America's "maddeningly complex" income-based tax system reinforces all four of these major structural imbalances. It discourages both savings and investment while handcuffing American exporters even as Washington's enormous power to tax promotes a cult of fiscal irresponsibility and monetary excess within the Beltway.

It's not just that our Federal income tax system reinforces the American economy's growth-stalling structural imbalances. The labyrinthine tax code's more than 60,000 pages also imposes a heavy "inefficiency tax." The facts are startling:

American taxpayers now collectively spend over 3.5 *billion* hours a year on tax preparation, and the cost of America's tax compliance is a staggering $150 billion. This epic waste totals more than combined federal government spending annually on agriculture, education, energy, environmental protection, NASA, and homeland security. Taken together, the growth-stalling effects of the American tax system and its large inefficiency tax represent the very definition of insanity. Insanity is something you keep doing repeatedly—or, in this case, something you keep filing repeatedly—expecting a different result.

This insanity prevails despite studies by economists such as Alan Auerbach of the University of California at Berkeley and the late David Bradford of Princeton University. They have found that fundamental reform such as changing to a consumption levy that taxes income only once could yield annual household income gains of up to 10%.

This insanity likewise prevails despite a wave of tax reform sweeping the globe. In the wake of that reform tsunami, America now has the highest corporate tax rate of any country save Japan—which has been in slow-growth mode for more than a decade. As shown in Exhibit 5.1, America now also has a statutory corporate tax rate that is fully 50% higher than the average for countries in the OECD.[1] Despite this high burden, the Obama administration has sought to further raise taxes on corporate capital.

Exhibit 5.1   OECD Nations Continue to Cut Corporate Tax Rates While the United States Stands Still (Statutory Rates, Federal Plus Provincial and State, 2007 and 2008)

Rank	Country	Corporate Tax Rate 2008	Corporate Tax Rate 2007	Change from 2007 to 2008
1	Japan	39.54	39.54	0
2	United States	39.25	39.26	0
3	France	34.43	34.43	0
4	Belgium	33.99	33.99	0
5	Canada	33.5	36.12	−2.6
6	Luxembourg	30.38	30.38	0
7	Germany	30.18	38.9	−8.7
8	Australia	30	30	0
9	New Zealand	30	33	−3
10	Spain	30	32.5	−2.5
11	Mexico	28	28	0
12	Norway	28	28	0
13	Sweden	28	28	0
14	United Kingdom	28	30	−2
15	Italy	27.5	33	−5.5
16	Korea	27.5	27.5	0
17	Portugal	26.5	26.5	0
18	Finland	26	26	0
19	Netherlands	25.5	25.5	0
20	Austria	25	25	0
21	Denmark	25	25	0
22	Greece	25	25	0
23	Switzerland	21.17	21.32	−0.1
24	Czech Republic	21	24	−3
25	Hungary	20	20	0

Exhibit 5.1   OECD Nations Continue to Cut Corporate Tax Rates While the United States Stands Still (Statutory Rates, Federal Plus Provincial and State, 2007 and 2008)

Rank	Country	Corporate Tax Rate 2008	Corporate Tax Rate 2007	Change from 2007 to 2008
26	Turkey	20	20	0
27	Poland	19	19	0
28	Slovak Republic	19	19	0
29	Iceland	15	18	−3
30	Ireland	12.5	12.5	0
	OECD average	26.6	27.6	−1

Source: The Tax Foundation[2]

Ideological Gridlock Over Broad-based Tax Reform

The failure of the United States to engage in broad-based tax reform—even as much of the rest of the world seems to have gotten the message—is in many ways a failure of both Democrats and Republicans to escape their own myopic ideologies. On the Left, many Democrats have fallen in love with taxing both "the rich" and "big business," oblivious to the growth-stalling effects of onerous taxes on savings, investment, entrepreneurship, and job creation.

On the Right, many Republicans simply want to slash taxes in the current broken system rather than acknowledge the need for a certain level of government revenues and the need to boldly reform the tax-collecting system. Often, too, in a frontal assault on the progressiveness of the American tax system, many Republicans demand that marginal tax rates in the current system be "flattened"—when the real solution is flattening the whole system with a steamroller and starting over.

In circling their ideological wagons, all that America's partisan politicians have managed to produce is an endless stream of tax preferences, loopholes, and full employment for the accounting and legal professions. Indeed, since the last major tax reform, undertaken in 1986, more than 15,000 changes have been made to the tax code in over 100 separate acts of Congress. That's an average of more than two changes a day—which we need to put an end to.

The practical result of America's ideological "tax wars" typically has been tax hikes whenever the Democrats ascend to power and tax cuts when the Republicans grab it back—never any real, broad-based reform. This destructive pattern is painfully evident in the stark contrast between the Bush and Obama White Houses.

After George W. Bush took office in 2001, his efforts to undertake a major reform of the tax system were sharply rebuffed. In lieu of such real reform, the Bush White House at least reduced marginal individual and corporate income tax rates while reducing taxes on capital gains and dividends—but only under the proviso that these tax cuts would expire in 2010.

In allowing some of the Bush tax cuts to expire, President Obama has effectively raised statutory marginal tax rates across the board for households. Moreover, from a GDP Growth Driver and Ten Levers of Growth perspective, the worst news from the Obama White House has been for business investment. With the expiration of the Bush tax cuts, the long-term capital gains tax rate will rise by one-third (to 20% from 15%), and the top tax rate on dividends will nearly triple (to 39.6% from 15%).

In addition, ObamaCare (discussed in more detail in Chapter 8, "Cutting the Gordian Knot of Entitlements") will slap on an additional 3.8% tax on so-called "unearned income"—capital gains, interest income, and dividends—starting in 2013. This means that the total Obama tax hike on capital will be 8.8 percentage points—an almost 60% jump.

On top of this, the estate tax will roar back from extinction, with a top rate of 55% and an exempt amount of only $600,000 (although some compromise may lower the tax rate and raise the exemption somewhat). Finally, the alternative minimum tax will reach far deeper into the middle class, ensnaring 25 million largely middle-class tax filers in its web.

Taken together, President Obama's "passive-aggressive" approach to raising taxes—letting the Bush cuts expire and instituting an ObamaCare capital tax—will drive up the personal income tax burden by more than 25%. As shown in Exhibit 5.2, this is the highest point relative to the GDP in U.S. experience.

Exhibit 5.2   The Largest Tax Increase Since World War II

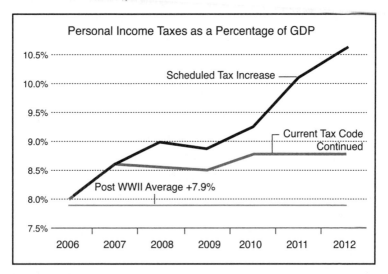

Source: Office of Management and Budget

From a historical perspective, the Obama tax hikes will also result in the largest increase in personal income taxes since World War II. The hikes are more than twice as large as President Lyndon Johnson's surcharge to finance the war in Vietnam and the war on poverty. They are also more than twice the combined personal income tax increases under Presidents George H.W. Bush and Bill Clinton.

The taxing news doesn't stop here. By running large budget deficits, President Obama is virtually ensuring major tax increases down the road that will inevitably slow growth. Already, the president has either passed or considered tax hikes that include raising individual income tax rates, increasing tax rates on multinational companies, and, as noted, applying Medicare taxes to investment income to fund new health care spending.

Most broadly, the Obama strategy of ratifying spending with higher taxes will require that all federal taxes rise by nearly 60%. This will bring the tax burden level to that of Europe's perennially slow-growing welfare state.

The "Seeds of Destruction" tragedy here is that even as our economy continues to lack the requisite horsepower to significantly reduce our historically high unemployment rates, politicians from both sides of the aisle remain oblivious to the fact that one of the best ways to get this country moving again is to engage in broad-based tax reform.

From a "Class Tax" to a "Mass Tax"

Given the compelling need for broad-based tax reform, the question we must turn to now is this: What should any such reform look like? To answer that question, it's useful to first briefly review the history and basic structure of our current income tax-based system.

In this regard, you may be surprised to learn that the American income tax got its start in 1913 not as a tax on all Americans but rather as a "class tax" on the ultra-rich. In fact, this original American income tax targeted only the top 1% of earners.

That all changed in the 1930s, when the government began with-holding payroll taxes to fund one of the most important social welfare programs of Franklin Delano Roosevelt's New Deal—Social Security. Once World War II started, the federal income tax was turned up several more notches as it was used to help finance the war.

By the end of World War II, almost 75% of Americans were subject to the income tax, compared with only 5% in 1939.[3] By this time, "the income tax had been transformed from a 'class tax' on the wealthier Americans into a 'mass tax' paid by most Americans to fund what had become a substantially larger federal government."[4]

Exhibit 5.3 is a pie chart of the various sources of tax revenue that the federal government relies on. As shown, the personal income tax provides 45% of all revenues, and the corporate income tax contributes another 13%. When contributions to Social Security are excluded from the total, the federal income tax contributes over 90% of all tax revenues. Clearly—and unlike the vast majority of its competitor nations—the United States relies heavily on its income tax.

Exhibit 5.3   The Tax Revenue "Pie" of the Federal Government

Federal Tax Revenues

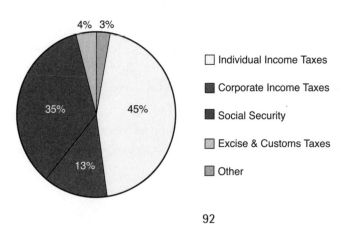

From Double Taxation to Double Whammies

From the vantage point of the GDP Growth Drivers equation and our Ten Levers of Growth, inherent, fundamental flaws within the American income tax-based system will virtually ensure that the American economy will lag behind its competitors in the decades ahead—unless broad-based reform is undertaken.

First and foremost, the entire incentive structure of the income tax is counterproductive—and counter to higher productivity. By taxing earnings rather than consumption, the system penalizes effort rather than rewarding saving and investment. So right off the bat, any income tax-based system will be inferior to a consumption tax system when it comes to stimulating growth, entrepreneurship, and job creation.

Second, and more specifically, America's income tax system is riddled with "double taxation" traps. These traps discourage the export-led growth and capital formation necessary to spur technological change and productivity growth.

Consider, for example, the double taxation of capital income. A corporation is first taxed on any profits it earns. When the corporation then distributes some of those profits to shareholders in the form of dividends, the individual shareholder is also taxed on such capital income.

This particular form of "double taxation" leads to a "double whammy" for investment. The corporate profits tax reduces the after-tax rate of return on new investment and thereby reduces the level of investment that would otherwise exist in the absence of the tax.

The personal income tax on dividends similarly reduces the after-tax rate of return on capital investment and thereby reduces the amount of capital that individuals might otherwise invest in the financial markets. This tax, in turn, raises the cost of capital and reduces investment.

Consider next the double taxation of American multinational corporations operating in foreign countries. Although multinationals are a common target of populist wrath, such corporations are an important conduit for selling exports to the rest of the world. Under the present tax code, not only do American corporations have to pay the taxes imposed by foreign governments, but they also must pay U.S. taxes if the foreign tax rate is less than the U.S. tax rate. The practical effect of such a tax regime is yet another "double whammy." First, American exporters are put at a competitive disadvantage to their foreign rivals. This form of double taxation also provides a strong incentive for multinationals to move their headquarters abroad—yet another blow to domestic business investment.

Finally, consider the double taxation of compensation itself. Uncle Sam first taxes us on our earnings. Then, if we save any portion of what's left over after taxes, any income we earn in interest, dividends, or capital gains is taxed again in a second wave. That's yet another disincentive to personal savings and investment.

A third major problem with our tax system is that it rewards precisely the kinds of behaviors that accentuate our structural imbalances. Consider the sacred cow of the mortgage interest rate deduction. The purpose of this deduction is to help Americans achieve the dream of homeownership—perhaps a laudable goal. However, although the almost unlimited nature of this deduction helps lower-income individuals buy their first home, it also encourages excessive investment in housing. It has likewise helped encourage precisely the kind of speculative behavior that led to the housing bubble.

A fourth major problem with the U.S. tax system is that it encourages corporate leverage. The problem is that, under the corporate income tax, businesses fully deduct their interest payments. This encourages the use of debt financing over equity financing. However, during recessions, when cash flows may be squeezed, corporations still have to make their interest payments and may be unable to service their debt. In this way, recessions—and the tax incentives for heavy debt financing in our current tax code—can drive corporations into bankruptcy.

The final major problem with our tax system is its complexity and the collateral heavy compliance burden it imposes on all of us. Nobody in this country should have to spend an average of 26 hours every year preparing their tax-return data. Yet every year, each of us— rich or poor and everyone in between—wastes precious family time on this onerous task. Sixty percent of us shell out hundreds of dollars or more for tax preparers, and another 25% fork over $50 or more for software so that we can prepare our own taxes.[5] This, too, is the very definition of insanity.

Income Tax Evolution or Consumption Tax Revolution?

"The key difference between an income tax and a consumption tax is a tax burden on capital income. An income tax includes capital income in the tax base, while a consumption tax does not. Taxing capital income reduces the return to savings and raises the cost of future consumption relative to current consumption. This is likely to cause people to spend more and save less, thereby depressing the level of capital accumulation."

President's Advisory Panel on Federal Tax Reform (2005)

In thinking about broad-based tax reform, any plan should seek to broaden the tax base, reduce marginal tax rates, and, most important from a growth-stimulating perspective, remove any tax incentives against savings, investment, entrepreneurial risk-taking, and exports. In looking at specific reforms, three main alternatives must be considered. Each one was carefully analyzed by the bipartisan 2005 President's Advisory Panel on Federal Tax Reform.

The most radical and revolutionary reform would scrap the income tax system and replace it with the purest form of a consumption tax. This change could take the form of either a national retail sales tax or, more likely, a "value-added tax" (VAT).

One problem with a national sales tax is that it would be highly regressive. In other words, lower-income individuals would pay a much greater share of their income in taxes than higher-income individuals. In addition, because tax rates would have to rise fairly significantly to raise the requisite revenue—as high as 30% or more—a retail sales tax would also invite various forms of tax evasion. For these reasons, a national retail sales tax is generally viewed as a political nonstarter.

An only slightly more palatable alternative is the VAT. With a VAT, revenues are collected in small increments throughout the production process and thereby have less-visible effects on the final consumer. Or the tax could be imposed on business revenue, less purchases from other firms, making this tax easy to administer.

In fact, most industrialized countries around the world have adopted some form of VAT. One frequently voiced criticism, however, is that "introducing a VAT would lead to higher total tax collections over time and facilitate the development of a larger federal government—in other words ... the VAT could be a 'money machine.'"[6] For this reason alone, many fiscal conservatives have a hard time embracing the VAT concept. Given that one of the biggest problems facing the United States right now is uncontrolled government spending, this type of criticism likely makes the VAT politically difficult as well.

If a radical consumption tax revolution with a retail sales tax or VAT will not occur, what is available at the other end of the more evolutionary reform spectrum?

One approach examined by the President's Advisory Panel embodies a "blended" income and consumption tax approach. This approach, described in the Panel's Growth and Investment Tax Plan, gently overhauls the current income tax while embedding it with certain consumption tax-like features.

For individuals, this blended plan cuts in half the number of tax brackets and reduces the highest marginal tax rate. It also reduces—but does not eliminate—the tax rate on dividends, capital gains, and interest.

For businesses, this plan likewise reduces the marginal tax rate. It also allows expensing for all new investment and removes the deductibility for interest payments while providing for international border tax adjustments.

The practical effect of such a plan would be to significantly increase savings and capital formation and the economic and wage growth that come with it. However, *because this approach does not eliminate the double taxation of capital income or the biases against savings and investment, it does not go far enough.*

Meeting on the Middle Ground

Between the radical step of a pure consumption tax such as a national retail sales tax or a VAT and the gradualism of a "blended" income and consumption tax system like that of the Growth and Investment Tax Plan, we believe a solid middle ground exists where taxpayers in this country can comfortably stand. This middle ground is embodied in a "progressive consumption tax" proposed by many leading economists and also examined by the President's Advisory Panel.

The progressive consumption tax takes the blended approach one giant step further *by fully rewarding saving and capital investment*. For individuals, income continues to be taxed with a progressive rate structure. However, all forms of capital income earned by individuals—interest, dividends, and capital gains—are exempt.

For businesses, corporate profits likewise continue to be taxed. However, all capital investment is fully expensed, while the deduction for interest payments on capital investment is eliminated.

In these ways, a progressive consumption tax provides maximum incentives for individuals to save and for businesses to invest. Eliminating the interest deduction for businesses also eliminates the bias against equity financing and thereby provides for a more stable capital structure during business cycle downturns.

We strongly prefer such a progressive consumption tax system because of its superior economic and political characteristics. From a political perspective, maintaining the progressivity of the American tax structure is a critical—indeed, essential—component of any political consensus on tax reform.

In fact, any progressive consumption tax reform can be done to ensure that the new system is "progressivity-neutral" with respect to the old system. This statement simply requires broadening the tax base and applying tax credits for low- and middle-income households. In this way, the test of "progressivity neutrality" can be achieved just as easily as "revenue neutrality"—a second critical political element of any reform.

From an economic point of view, a progressive consumption tax is likewise compelling. It meets the most important challenge of stimulating growth by providing maximum incentives for individual savings and business investment while removing the double taxation of capital income.

A progressive consumption tax approach is also fully consistent with the findings of a recent study by the OECD. It found that "corporate taxes are found to be most harmful for growth, followed by personal income taxes, and then consumption taxes."[7] This study also found that "If countries want to enhance their economic growth, they would do well to move away from income taxes—especially corporate income taxes—toward less distortive taxes such as consumption-based taxes" and "The key to creating a growth-oriented corporate income tax system is to impose a reasonably low tax rate with few exemptions."[8]

The compelling need for such a broad-based progressive consumption tax reform cannot be overestimated. America's current tax system is a train wreck when it comes to capital formation, job creation, and long-term economic growth. Indeed, every incentive of the current system points in the wrong direction. As we have seen, this system merely exacerbates, rather than ameliorates, the four major structural imbalances in our GDP Growth Driver equation.

In fact, the estimated gains from adopting a progressive consumption tax would be significant. The U.S. Treasury Department estimates that such a reform would increase national income by up to 6% over the long run—about $800 billion annually at current real GDP levels. It also would increase the capital stock, which measures the economy's accumulation of wealth, by as much as 28%.[9] These gains would translate into millions of new jobs created and substantial increases in wages and income.

Just what are we waiting for?

Endnotes

1. Scott Hodge. "OECD Finds Corporate Taxes Most Harmful to Economic Growth." The Tax Foundation. August 13, 2008. http://www.taxfoundation.org/blog/show/23478.html.

2. http://www.taxfoundation.org/news/show/23470.html.

3. The President's Advisory Panel on Federal Tax Reform (2005), p. 12.

4. This quotation, as well as the brief history, comes from The President's Advisory Panel on Federal Tax Reform, p. 12.

5. The President's Advisory Panel on Federal Tax Reform, pp. 2-3.

6. The President's Advisory Panel on Federal Tax Reform, p.192.

7. Scott Hodge. The relevant OECD study is "Tax and Economic Growth," Economics Department Working Paper No. 620, July 11, 2008. Organization for Economic Cooperation and Development, p. 9. http://www.olis.oecd.org/olis/2008doc.nsf/LinkTo/NT00003502/$FILE/JT03248896.PDF.

8. Ibid.

9. The President's Advisory Panel on Federal Tax Reform, p. 190.

chapter six

Why the Best "Jobs Program" May Be Trade Reform

"Foreign producers receive subsidies, tax abatements, free buildings, free energy. They do not pay taxes. They don't have to pay Social Security, workman's comp, disability or health care. They don't have to match a 401(k) contribution. They are able to avoid more than 100 years of government regulations put on American businesses. OSHA does not exist in most developing nations. They use electricity that would never be allowed to be generated in the United States due to lack of pollution controls. The U.S. Environmental Protection Agency employs 17,000 workers. China's state environmental protection administration employs only 300."

R. McCormack, *Manufacturing a Better Future for America* (2009)

One of the most powerful insights of the GDP Growth Driver analysis described in Chapter 2, "How to Lift the American Economy with the Ten Levers of Growth," is that large and chronic trade deficits can stall the American economy. Recall from that chapter that in our benchmark period from 1946 to 1999, the American economy grew, on average, more than 3.2% annually. During that period, American trade with the rest of the world had no net negative impact on GDP growth. Net exports were near 0% and therefore did not subtract from GDP growth, and America was able to grow at its full potential growth rate.

During the nought decade of the 2000s, however, as our trade deficit grew to record proportions, the average negative impact of net exports on total annual GDP jumped to fully –5%. It may have reduced our annual GDP growth rate by as much as 0.5%. The result was a collateral loss of millions of jobs that otherwise might have been created in our domestic manufacturing and export industries.

If we want to reduce America's large and chronic trade deficits—and thereby return to the path of long-term prosperity—there are really only two major ways to do so. We need to reduce America's heavy oil import dependence and shrink America's trade imbalance, particularly with our largest trading partner, China. This claim is quite evident in Exhibit 6.1. It illustrates that oil imports and America's "China deficit" account for 41% and 45% of our trade deficit in goods, respectively—an astonishing 86% of the total deficit (excluding services)![1] This chapter looks at how to rebalance our trade with China, and the next chapter examines how to best reduce America's oil import dependence.

Exhibit 6.1   Major Sources of America's Chronic Trade Deficits (2009)

	Trade Balance (in Billions of Dollars)	Trade Balance by Percentage of Total
U.S. petroleum imports balance	–204	41%
U.S.–China trade balance	–227	45%
Total net exports	–501	

Source: United States Department of Commerce, Bureau of Economic Analysis

The 2000s: A Decade of Large and Chronic Trade Deficits

To set the stage for our discussion about how to reduce America's large and chronic trade deficits, Exhibit 6.2 illustrates their explosive growth. You can see that although the annual U.S. trade deficit began to rapidly expand as far back as 1992, it more than doubled in the nought decade, from around $30 billion a year in 2000 to almost $70 billion by 2006.

Exhibit 6.2   Chronic Trade Imbalances Double in the Nought Decade

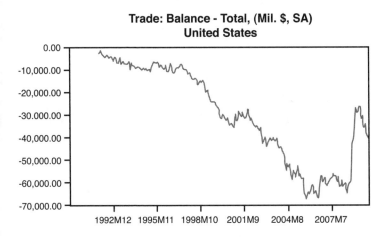

You can also see that beginning in 2008, our trade deficit fell sharply—but this was hardly good news. Instead, this apparent "improvement" in the trade balance was simply an artifact of the financial crisis and the Great Recession of 2007–2009. This economic downturn led to sharply reduced trade volumes and at least a temporary reprieve from high oil prices. However, as the U.S. economy has begun to recover, America's trade gap with the rest of the world is again widening.

America's Trade Deficits Cause Inflation and Loss of Political Sovereignty

America's chronic trade deficits do not just lead to slower GDP growth than we could otherwise achieve. They also put significant downward pressure on the dollar and thereby can create inflationary problems. In this regard, although a cheaper dollar helps boost U.S. exports, a weaker dollar also causes domestic inflation because it raises the cost of imported goods—from Hondas and Audis to flat-panel TVs and foreign oil.

As a longer-term strategic threat, America's chronic trade deficits have also led to a dangerous buildup of U.S. dollar reserves in countries that, in turn, have sought to use their holdings of such reserves to influence U.S. policies. A fascinating case in point is offered by former Treasury Secretary Henry Paulson.

In Paulson's financial crisis memoir *On the Brink*, he reveals how Russia urged China to dump its holdings in Fannie Mae and Freddie Mac bonds in 2008. Russia intended such a financial attack to force the Treasury Department to bail out these government-sponsored mortgage-finance companies to preserve the value of Russia's holdings in them—holdings that were priced at up to $100 billion.[2]

To Paulson, the report of Russia's disruptive attacks to influence American policy was "deeply troubling." This is because "heavy selling could create a sudden loss of confidence ... and shake the capital markets."[3]

The World's Poster Child for the Modern Protectionist-Mercantilist State

Given that America's chronic trade deficits act as a brake on growth, are inflationary, and raise difficult issues related to a loss of America's political sovereignty, our next question is this: How can the United States reduce its chronic trade imbalances with China—its largest trading partner?

In thinking about how to answer this question, it's useful to begin with another: Why does America buy so much more from China than China buys from America?

One possibility is that China's labor is simply much cheaper and that Chinese enterprises are simply much more efficient than American businesses. If this is the explanation, the only way America can reduce its trade deficit with China in a world of free and fair trade is to learn how to compete better. And, of course, increased saving in the United States would help reduce the trade deficit generally.

In fact, there is some evidence that China's cheap but very well trained labor force is an important source of its competitive advantage. For example, in a year-long study conducted by one of us (Navarro), the Report of the China Price Project found that cheap labor contributed a little more than 40% of the production cost advantage that Chinese enterprises have over their foreign competitors.[4]

However, other findings of the China Price Project also raised another possibility. This is that China runs large trade imbalances with the United States because it zealously protects its markets from U.S. imports even as it uses a wide range of mercantilist practices to "beggar its neighbors."

In fact, the China Price Project also found that five particularly unfair trade practices collectively were just as important as cheap labor in honing China's competitive edge. These practices included illegal export subsidies, an undervalued currency, counterfeiting and piracy, and lax environmental and health and safety standards. In a companion study, Navarro also found that China engages in an elaborate web of protectionist and mercantilist activities that together give

Chinese enterprises a formidable advantage over world rivals—in clear violation of free trade principles.[5]

China's Great Wall of Protectionism

"China's state-owned railway system ... isn't allowed to use foreign technology. The reason is a desire to build up Chinese companies into national champions.... The restrictions go beyond internal regulations. Last week, China passed a new postal law that bans foreign companies from delivering express mail inside China, a blow to FedEx Corp. of the U.S. and Germany's DHL Worldwide Express Inc., which have lobbied for years against the new rules. China also maintains rules openly limiting foreign investment in key sectors, such as autos, chemicals and information technologies."

Wall Street Journal (April 2009)[6]

Exhibit 6.3 is an overview of the most important protectionist policies employed as part of China's broader industrial policy strategy. Note that each of these protectionist measures violates conditions that China agreed to for its accession to the World Trade Organization (WTO) in 2001.

In the arena of protectionist *tariffs and quotas*, China continues to maintain significant tariffs on a wide range of industries, from air conditioners, refrigerators, and washing machines to cameras, copying machines, electronic calculators, furniture, and foodstuffs. China also imposes particularly stiff tariffs to protect so-called "pillar industries" such as motor vehicles.

Consider, for example, China's massive motorcycle market, in which more than 25 million units are sold annually. If a company such as America's Harley Davidson wants to export into this lucrative

Exhibit 6.3   China's Major Protectionist Policies Sharpen Its Competitive Edge

Protectionist Policy	Description
Quotas and tariffs	Quotas set numeric limits on imports to directly restrict imports.
	Tariffs tax imports and indirectly restrict imports through pricing.
Local content rules ("buy domestic")	Require Chinese local, state, and central governments and domestic industries to use domestic content, thereby effectively locking out foreign competitors.
Import licensing restrictions	Import licenses are required to do business in China but are very hard to get. Provision of licenses often is used as a "bargaining chip" to impose local content rules, force technology transfer, and force offshoring of R&D to China.
Forced technology transfer	Require technology transfer and/or the export of a country's R&D facilities as a condition of market entry.
	Steal or reverse-engineer technology through industrial espionage in violation of patent law.
Technical barriers to trade	The use of discriminatory regulations, standards and certification, and testing procedures to benefit domestic industries at the expense of foreign exporters.
Discriminatory tax policies	Consumption, income, and other tax policies that favor domestic industries, such as income tax refunds for the purchase of local content.
Corruption and bribery	Rigged bidding and other corrupt practices often favor domestic industries.
Port-of-entry restrictions	Used to block, slow down, or otherwise impede the flow of imports into the domestic market at ports of entry.
Inflated customs valuations	Used to inflate the price of an import using spurious customs valuation methods and thereby raise the associated import duties. Often used to offset tariff reductions.

Chinese market, it must contend with both a stiff 30% tariff and the imposition of additional value-added and consumption taxes.

An equally interesting example, which illustrates how protectionism forces foreign manufacturers to offshore their production to China, is China's "back door" tariff on its highly lucrative domestic automobile parts industry. As noted by Global Europe, when China joined the WTO, it agreed to treat auto parts as different from "complete vehicles" and impose no more than a 10% tariff. However, China continues to impose a much higher 25% duty on specific combinations of imported parts, even when those parts do not in any way constitute a completed vehicle. In this way, "the rules oblige EU car makers who wish to avoid higher duties to source car parts in China."[7]

Even when China has lowered tariffs on some products, often it has sought to offset any tariff reductions with a potent array of non-tariff barriers. For example, China's *local content rules* require all layers of government—local, regional, and national—to give priority to goods and services of Chinese origin. In fact, "many of China's provinces, which have as many as 100 million inhabitants, are run like individual countries, with rules banning purchases outside the province," and "many provinces have lists of products that must be bought inside the province."[8]

The Chinese government also orders many of its private industries—particularly pillar industries such as autos and telecommunications—to "buy domestic." Partly on the strength of local content rules and steep protective tariffs, China has traveled at warp speed from a country with an extremely small and undeveloped auto and auto parts industry to become the third-largest automobile producer in the world and the second-largest auto parts supplier to the U.S. market.[9]

Still another protectionist tool in China's complex game of "hide the tariff" is its creative uses of *import licensing restrictions*. Under the Chinese system, overseas exporters must apply for the right to export to the Chinese market. If the license is denied—as is often the case—companies must wait for fully three years before they can reapply.

Besides blocking market access, the issuance of import licenses is often used as an important "bargaining chip" to coerce American and other foreign companies operating in China to adopt local content rules. In addition, as a condition of receiving a license, foreign companies often have to agree to transfer their technology to Chinese companies and even offshore some of their R&D investment directly to Chinese soil. Here's how this particular protectionist tool has helped build China's auto industry, even as employment in America's auto industry has shrunk by more than 50% over the past decade:

China first limits the number of licenses granted for final automobile assembly. American and other foreign automakers then must compete for the licenses. Of course, the winners of this competition are the companies that are most willing to agree to local content rules, to transfer their technology, and to locate more R&D on Chinese soil. (See the sidebar at the end of this chapter.)

As Professor Eric Thun of Princeton has described this coercive process: "foreign firms, desperate not to be locked out of one of the last great auto markets ... claw over one another to get the contract."[10] The significance of these types of transfers of technology for America's trade deficit and long-term U.S. growth prospects has been noted by GlobalSecurity.org:

"Technology transfer is both mandated in Chinese regulations or industrial policies (with which U.S. companies wishing to invest in China must comply) and used as a deal-maker or sweetener by U.S. firms seeking joint venture contracts in China. Unless significant changes are made to China's current investment regulations and import/export policies, U.S. commercial technology transfers to China are likely to continue, potentially enhancing Chinese competitiveness in high-technology industry sectors such as aerospace and electronics. The U.S.–China trade imbalance may continue to worsen in the short term as commercial offset demands and foreign-invested enterprise exports increase and in the long term as China's plans to develop indigenous capabilities in both basic and advanced technology industries are implemented."[11]

A typical case in point involves General Motors—a company that the American taxpayer has been forced to bail out with billions of tax dollars because of its flagging domestic operations. Not only has GM "been a major conduit of technology"[12] to China, but in exchange for licenses, GM also "has committed to purchasing $10 billion annually in Chinese-produced auto parts," Moreover, Ford also has "made at least $3 billion in commitments to buying substantial quantities of Chinese-produced parts for export to four plants worldwide."[13]

On top of all these various protectionist tools, China uses various *technical barriers to trade*. Chief among them is China's mandating of unique national standards such as its own version of a cell phone 3G standard. These national standards are mandated despite the existence of well established international standards. In effect, they serve as a shield for a wide range of domestic industries that include automobiles and automotive parts, telecommunications equipment and wireless local area networks, radio frequency identification technology and audio and video coding, fertilizers and food products, and even consumer products such as cosmetics.[14]

The bottom line is that it is very difficult for American corporations to penetrate China's Great Walls of Protectionism. Even when American corporations are allowed into China's markets, they often are forced or coerced into surrendering their technology. As Chapter 2, which discussed the Ten Levers of Growth, taught us, this loss of technology and R&D investment to China is likely to take a significant toll on the rate of American innovation and growth.

China's Eighteenth Century Mercantilism

"China has become a major financial and trade power. But it doesn't act like other big economies. Instead, it follows a mercantilist policy, keeping its trade surplus artificially high. And in today's depressed world, that policy is, to put it bluntly, predatory."

Nobel Laureate Economist Paul Krugman,
New York Times (December 2009)[15]

Even as China employs a sophisticated suite of policies to protect its domestic markets, it uses an equally potent array of mercantilist tools to gain advantage over foreign competitors such as the United States. At the top of the list of these mercantilist tools, described in Exhibit 6.4, is China's complex web of *export subsidies.*

Exhibit 6.4   China's Major Mercantilist Policies Beggar Its Neighbors

Mercantilist Policy	Description
Export subsidies	*Direct* export subsidies such as discriminatory tax rates on exported goods. *Indirect* export subsidies through the subsidization of inputs such as capital, energy, freight, land, water, and other utilities.
Currency manipulation	Undervalue the domestic currency to make "exports cheap" and "imports dear."
Counterfeiting and piracy	Counterfeiting reduces marketing and production costs to hone competitive advantage. Piracy reduces R&D and information technology costs.
Lax environmental and health and safety regulations	Maintain environmental and health and safety regulations far below international norms to reduce compliance and production costs for Chinese manufacturers. Encourages a "race to the bottom."
Export restrictions	Restrict the export of energy or raw materials to suppress factor input prices in the mercantilist country and raise world market prices for competitors.

China's Illegal Export Subsidies Are Not WTO-Compliant

China's web of *illegal export subsidies* continues to exist almost a decade after China joined the WTO and agreed to eliminate that web. Today, according to the U.S. Trade Representative, the industries that continue to be hardest hit by China's export subsidies include "steel, petrochemicals, high technology, forestry and paper products, textiles, hardwood plywood, machinery, copper, and other nonferrous metals industries."[16]

Likewise, according to the U.S. Trade Representative, what makes it extremely challenging for American industries to individually fight back in the legal arena against Chinese export subsidies is "a general lack of transparency" that "makes it difficult to identify and quantify possible export subsidies provided by the Chinese government."[17]

Although the exact levels of China's export subsidies remain difficult to quantify, it is relatively easy to catalogue them. First, energy and water remain heavily subsidized,[18] and many manufacturers also benefit from subsidized rent and cheap or free land.

Second, China's state-owned banks continue to hold a large portfolio of nonperforming loans. These nonperforming loans represent a major subsidy because borrowers neither make their interest payments nor repay the loan's principal. The biggest beneficiaries of this "free money" have been state-owned enterprises that are concentrated in heavy industries such as steel and petroleum.

A third vehicle to subsidize exports is China's discriminatory tax system. Consider, for example, the China-Singapore Suzhou Industrial Park, which is typical of China's Special Economic Zones. The long list of tax incentives available to exporters includes a 50% cut in the income tax rate; a local income tax exclusion; full tax exemptions in the first two years; tax cuts on dividends, interest, rental, royalty, and other incomes; and refundable taxes on any water, power, and gas purchased by firms producing for export.[19] On the basis of these tax breaks alone, it's no wonder that companies from Michigan, Ohio, California, or Pennsylvania have difficulty competing against their Chinese counterparts.

China's Undervalued Currency Perpetuates Trade Imbalances

"I conclude that the renminbi is undervalued, that this is danger-ous for the durability of global recovery, and that China's actions have not, so far, provided a durable solution. I conclude, too, that rebalancing is a necessary condition for sustainable recovery, changes in competitiveness are a necessary condition for rebal-ancing, real renminbi appreciation is necessary for changes in competitiveness, and a rise in the currency is necessary for real appreciation, given the Chinese desire to curb inflation. The United States was right to give talking a chance. But talk must now lead to action."

Martin Wolf, *Financial Times* (April 2010)[20]

In addition to China's complex web of export subsidies is the equally potent mercantilist tool of China's *currency manipulation*. We dis-cussed this issue at length in Chapters 2 and 5, so we will be brief here. Suffice it to say that by virtually all creditable estimates, the Chinese yuan (also known as the *renminbi*) is considerably underval-ued—in the range of 20% to 40%.

Martin Wolf's observations, noted previously, perfectly encapsu-late the wide range of issues involved in an undervaluation of the yuan. As noted by the U.S.–China Economic and Security Review Commission, "China's undervalued currency encourages undervalued Chinese exports to the U.S. and discourages U.S. exports because U.S. exports are artificially overvalued."[21] This further observation from

Wolf in the *Financial Times* is likewise worth citing because it removes any doubt about China's intent with respect to its exchange rate:

> "China has controlled the appreciation of both nominal and real exchange rates. This surely is currency manipulation. It is also protectionist, being equivalent to a uniform tariff and an export subsidy."[22]

The far bigger problem with China's undervalued currency is not the competitive price advantage it provides to Chinese exporters *per se*. Rather, it is that by effectively pegging the yuan to the U.S. dollar, China makes it virtually impossible for America to reduce its massive trade deficit with China through exchange rate adjustments.

In this regard, as noted in Chapter 2, in a world of free trade characterized by floating exchange rates, the U.S.–China trade imbalance could never persist. As the U.S. trade deficit rose, the dollar would fall relative to the yuan, U.S. exports to China would rise, Chinese imports would fall, and trade would come back into balance. China, however, subverts this free-trade adjustment process—and the broader global free-trade system—with its fixed exchange rate.

China's Counterfeiting and Piracy Cut Production and R&D Costs

China is certainly not the only country to engage in *counterfeiting* and *piracy*. However, China accounts for an estimated two-thirds of all the world's pirated and counterfeited goods and 80% of all counterfeit goods seized at U.S. borders.

China's counterfeiting and piracy are very important drivers of its economic growth. In fact, Professor Oded Shenkar at Ohio University's Fisher School of Business estimates that intellectual property theft contributes anywhere from 10% to 30% of China's total GDP growth.[23]

To understand how Chinese counterfeiting and piracy help contribute to the U.S. trade deficit, it is critical to first note that such intellectual property theft extends far beyond Hollywood movies and fashion items such as Louis Vuitton bags. As the U.S. Trade Representative notes, affected industries include "software, pharmaceuticals, chemicals, information technology, apparel, athletic footwear, textile fabrics and floor coverings, consumer goods, food and beverages, electrical equipment, automotive parts and industrial products, among many others."[24]

Counterfeiting and piracy give Chinese enterprises an unfair competitive advantage by significantly reducing the costs of everything from R&D and marketing to information technology. Consider, for example, that the rate of software piracy in China is well over 90%. This provides substantial savings.

In addition, Chinese counterfeiters incur neither significant R&D expenditures nor substantial advertising and marketing costs. As noted by the consulting firm A.T. Kearney, "counterfeiting allows skipping the investment necessary to create, develop, and market products and go directly to profits. No R&D headaches. No brand building. No advertising."[25]

Chinese counterfeiting and piracy have a particularly sharp competitive edge in industries that are very R&D-intensive, such as autos, biotechnology, semiconductors, and pharmaceuticals. In such industries, R&D costs range as high as 15% of total revenues or more. Chinese exporters that do not have to bear these R&D costs thereby gain a significant competitive edge.

Pollution's Perverse Competitive Edge

In the space of three short decades in which China has emerged as the world's "factory floor," that country also has earned the dubious distinction of being the most polluted country on the planet. In fact,

lax environmental regulations give Chinese businesses another significant competitive advantage over American and other foreign competitors, which must abide by a far stricter set of regulations.

China's "pollution edge" cuts the deepest with precisely those
manufacturing industries in the United States that face the highest
compliance costs. Consider that companies such as Dow Chemical
and U.S. Steel spend about 3% of their revenues on environmental
expenses. By comparison, Chinese competitors such as Sinopec
Petroleum and Chemical and Bao Steel spend only about one-tenth as
much.

Chinese citizens pay a very high price for this particular mercantilist advantage. China is now home to 16 of the world's 20 most polluted cities. Of China's almost 100 cities with over a million people
each, two-thirds fail to meet World Health Organization air quality
standards.

The statistics on water pollution are equally stark. Seventy percent of China's seven major rivers are severely polluted, and 80% fail
to meet standards for fishing.[26] Ninety percent of China's cities and
75% of its lakes suffer from some degree of water pollution,[27] and 700
million Chinese "have access to drinking water of a quality below
World Health Organization standards."[28] The worst polluting industries—and those that gain the greatest "pollution edge" over
American competitors—include paper and pulp, food, chemicals, textiles, tanning, and mining. The most common toxic pollutants include
dioxins; solvents; PCBs; various metals such as mercury, lead, and
copper; and highly persistent pesticides ranging from chlordane and
mirex to DDT.[29]

Here's the irony of this situation, which has important implications for policy reform: Whatever China's environmental cost advantages are at the individual enterprise level, they are likely being
completely offset by the aggregate social costs of Chinese pollution.

The World Bank estimates that pollution annually costs China between 8% and 12% of its more than $1 trillion GDP because of increased medical bills, lost work due to illness, damage to fish and crops, and money spent on disaster relief.[30] These figures suggest that any cost-benefit analysis would favor China's cleaning up its environment rather than "racing to the bottom" to gain a mercantilist edge.

$$* \quad * \quad *$$

At this point, you might think we are picking on China too much. This is a legitimate point, but allow us to explain.

To begin, we again acknowledge that at least one important reason that China has been able to run a large trade surplus with the United States is because of America's very low saving rate and tendency toward overconsumption. In this sense, the U.S. consumption binge over much of the last decade has virtually guaranteed a trade deficit with some other country or countries, so America must share in the culpability for the situation it finds itself in.

That said, it is both necessary and appropriate to single out China in any discussion of reducing America's trade deficit. After all, China accounts for 45% of America's deficit in goods and fully 75% of the goods deficit once oil imports are excluded. China also engages in a wide range of protectionist and mercantilist practices that make it very difficult for American businesses to compete on a level free-trade playing field with China. The infamous Willie Sutton used to rob banks because "that's where the money is." Likewise, we must analyze the China trade because, through constructive trade reform and engagement with China, that is where America's best chance lies of reducing its non-oil-related trade deficit.

Beyond China, if the U.S. economy wants to reach its full potential GDP growth rate, it is equally critical that the United States boost its saving rate. It is also critical that the White House renew its leadership on behalf of a global free-trade agenda—a quality noticeably absent in the Obama administration.

As we noted in Chapter 2, during our analysis of the Ten Levers of Growth, the arguments in support of free trade that are based on the theory of "comparative advantage" have been familiar since the eighteenth century days of Adam Smith and David Ricardo. In this chapter, it is well worth noting further a large amount of recent empirical work that illustrates just how much countries can gain when they lower their trade barriers.

For example, Columbia professor Jeffrey Sachs and Andrew Warner of the World Bank found that in the 1970s and 1980s, open economies grew about 2.5% faster, on average, than more closed economies.[31] A second study by Harvard's Jeffrey Frankel and University of California–Berkeley's David Romer showed that raising a country's trade-to-GDP ratio by 1 percentage point raised income per capita by 2% or more.[32] Still a third study by the International Monetary Fund found that if the free-trade agenda were adopted worldwide, developing countries would profit enormously, with gains of about three times what they receive each year in aid.[33]

In pursuit of a free-trade agenda, both the president and Congress must emphasize that free trade means full compliance with WTO rules, the absence of any illegal export subsidies, a fairly valued currency, strict protection of intellectual property, the absence of any forced technology transfer, environmental and health and safety standards that meet international norms, free and open access to each country's domestic markets, and an unrestricted global market in raw materials.

Any nation that fails to follow these ground rules should be subject to appropriate defensive measures by the United States to safeguard the system of free trade and to ensure the long-term prosperity of the American economy. To put it another way, although the United

States needs to lead a global effort for free trade, our country cannot give large protectionist-mercantilist partners such as China a free pass. These general actions would improve both the U.S. trade position and economic growth.

HOW TECHNOLOGY TRANSFER MOVES CHINA UP THE VALUE CHAIN

A key element of China's industrial policy has been to move up the value chain rapidly from low-technology, lower-wage products such as toys and cheap electronics into high-value-added and higher-wage industries such as automobiles, aircraft, and pharmaceuticals. One of the most potent weapons China has used to move up the value chain is forced technology transfer. Only through the acquisition (rather than internal development) of sophisticated technologies have Chinese companies been able to rapidly enter and expand in sophisticated industries such as automobiles, aircraft, pharmaceuticals, and other high-tech areas.

Forced technology transfer is an extremely effective way for China to sharpen its competitive advantage, because China has a huge capability to "absorb and apply technology."[34] As noted by GlobalSecurity.org, "China has no shortage of well-trained scientists, engineers, mathematicians, or other technical experts, unlike the United States. Chinese scholars educated abroad over the last decade reportedly make up more than half of the top scientific researchers now working on key research projects and receiving priority in conducting this research."[35]

As noted in this chapter, China has very effectively used protectionist tools such as import licensing restrictions as "bargaining chips" to coerce technology transfer from automobile companies such as General Motors and Ford when they set up production facilities in China with the intention of selling into the Chinese market. The dynamic at work here is that "China is a buyer's market." The leverage of such an enormous potential market allows Chinese officials to frequently play foreign competitors against one another in their bids for joint venture contracts and large-scale, government-funded infrastructure projects in China. The typical result is usually more technology being transferred as competitors bid up the level or type of technology they are willing to offer.[36] In fact, "most U.S. and other foreign investors in China thus far seem willing to pay the price of technology transfers—even state-of-the-art technologies—in order to 'gain a foothold' or to 'establish a beachhead' in China with the expectation that the country's enormous market potential eventually will be realized."[37]

Beyond forced technology transfer, China also is using the offshoring of R&D facilities to China to gain important footholds in key high-value-added industries such as pharmaceuticals and aircraft. In the case of pharmaceuticals, in the initial phase of developing its domestic industries, China has used counterfeiting and pirating of prescription drugs such as Viagra and Lipitor to develop a large-scale manufacturing capability. And China has urged American pharmaceutical companies in China to set up R&D facilities in that country as a condition of market entry.

As for the aircraft industry, much of the technology that China has acquired for both its civilian and military aircraft production has been through industrial espionage. As noted by the Heritage Foundation, "China's official, government-sanctioned theft of advanced-technology intellectual property is another regular feature of China's industrial policy."[38]

It's not just the aircraft industry that has been subject to the theft of advanced technology. Chinese agents have been caught stealing, or attempting to steal, a wide variety of technologies from companies ranging from Cisco Systems and Sun Microsystems to NEC Electronics and Transmeta.[39] In a bold new front in Chinese espionage, Chinese hackers have begun launching cyber attacks on American corporations ranging from Adobe and Dow to Google. The goal of these attacks has been to probe for everything from trade secrets and technologies to client lists and marketing and distribution information.

A wide range of strategies to acquire new technologies and to force technology transfer is an important component of Chinese industrial policy—in violation of free-trade principles.

Endnotes

1. These statistics are based on 2009 data from the Department of Commerce. Excluding services provides a conservative estimate of the size of the petroleum and China effects on the U.S. balance of payments because the U.S. runs a net surplus in services in its trade balance—$132 billion in 2009. When services are included in the calculation, the share of petroleum imports rises to 55% of the total deficit (including both goods and services) and China's share rises to 61% of the total deficit—for a total of 116% of the total deficit.

2. Dow Jones Wire Service. "Russia Denies Paulson Claim of Plan to Sell Fannie Mae, Freddie Mac." February 1, 2010. As reported in this article, Russia subsequently denied any such attempt at this financial blackmail.

3. Michael McKee and Alex Nicholson. "Paulson Says Russia Urged China to Dump Fannie, Freddie Bonds." Bloomberg.com. January 29, 2010.

4. Peter Navarro. "The Economics of the China Price." *China Perspectives*. November-December, 2006.

5. Richard McCormack, editor. *Manufacturing a Better Future for America*. Alliance for American Manufacturing, 2009.

6. "Foreign Businesses Say China Is Growing More Protectionist." *Wall Street Journal*. April 28, 2009. http://online.wsj.com/article/ SB124082482232658755.html.

7. Global Europe. "Chinese tariffs on imports of EU car parts." Brussels. February 14, 2008. http://infoexport.gc.ca/eng/document. jsp?did=18005.

8. *Wall Street Journal*, April 28, 2009.

9. Andrew Szamosszegi. "How Chinese Government Subsidies and Market Intervention Have Resulted in the Offshoring of U.S. Auto Parts Production: A Case Study," p. 5.

10. Eric Thun. "Industrial policy, Chinese-style: FDI, regulation, and dreams of national champions in the auto sector." *Journal of East Asian Studies* (September–December 2004).

11. GlobalSecurity.org. "Weapons of Mass Destruction (WMD): Technology Transfer to China." http://www.globalsecurity.org/wmd/ library/report/1999/techtransfer2prc.htm.

12. Szamosszegi, p. 11.

13. Szamosszegi, p. 15. In a variation on this protectionist game, China threatened to double its tariffs on imported auto parts and components. In the ensuing negotiations, China agreed to postpone imposing the higher tariffs "but only after holding high-level meetings with the CEOs of BMW and DaimlerChrysler Northeast Asia. These meetings produced commitments to increase local parts purchases by $274 million and $740 million, respectively."

14. 2008 National Trade Estimate Report on Foreign Trade Barriers, Office of the United States Trade Representative (hereinafter, USTR Report). p. 91.

15. Paul Krugman. "Chinese New Year." *New York Times*. December 31, 2009.

16. USTR Report, p. 104.

17. Ibid.

18. Szamosszegi, p. 15. China's policy of offering free land use to multinationals has been particularly effective in attracting foreign direct investment.

19. Szamosszegi, pp. 20–22.

20. Martin Wolf, "Evaluating the renminbi manipulation." *Financial Times*, April 7, 2010.

21. "The Importance of Trade Remedies to the U.S. Trade Relationship with China." U.S.–China Economic and Security Review Commission. May 16, 2005.

22. Martin Wolf, April 7, 2010.

23. Oded Shenkar. *The Chinese Century: The Rising Chinese Economy and Its Impact on the Global Economy, the Balance of Power, and Your Job*. Upper Saddle River, NJ: Wharton School Publishing, 2006.

24. USTR Report, p. 111.

25. A.T. Kearney. "The Counterfeiting Paradox." http://www.atkearney.com/shared_res/pdf/Counterfeiting_Paradox.pdf.

26. Guang-Xin Zhang and Deng Wei. "The Groundwater Crisis and Sustainable Agriculture In Northern China." *Water Engineering and Management* (April 2002) 149(4): 13.

27. "China Says Water Pollution So Severe That Cities Could Lack Safe Supplies." *China Daily*. June 28, 2005.

28. Tina Butler. "China's Imminent Water Crisis." Mongabay.com. May 30, 2005. http://news.mongabay.com/2005/0531-tina_butler.html.

29. "Toxic Chemicals to be Phased Out." China.org.cn. November 11, 2004. http://www.china.org.cn/english/2004/Nov/111804.htm.

30. World Bank. "Clear Skies, Blue Water: China's Environment in the New Century." Washington, DC, 1997.

31. Jeffrey D. Sachs and Andrew Warner. "Economic Reform and the Process of Global Integration." *Brookings Papers on Economic Activity*, 1995(1): 1–95.

32. Jeffrey A. Frankel and David Romer. "Does Trade Cause Growth?" *American Economic Review*, June 1999, pp. 379–399.

33. International Monetary Fund. "Market Access for Developing Countries." Staff paper, 2001.

34. GlobalSecurity.org. "Weapons of Mass Destruction (WMD): Technology Transfer to China."

35. Ibid.

36. Ibid.

37. Ibid.

38. Heritage Foundation. "The U.S. Must Face Up to China's Trade Challenges." http://www.heritage.org/research/tradeandforeignaid/bg1698.cfm.

39. Ibid.

chapter seven

Why America's Foreign Oil Addiction Stunts Our Growth

"We will break the back of the energy crisis; we will lay the foundation for our future capacity to meet America's energy needs from America's own resources."

President Richard Nixon[1]

"We must end vulnerability to economic disruption by foreign [oil] suppliers by 1985."

President Gerald Ford[2]

"This intolerable dependence on foreign oil threatens our economic independence and the very security of our nation."

President Jimmy Carter[3]

"Keeping America competitive requires affordable energy. And here we have a serious problem: America is addicted to oil, which is often imported from unstable parts of the world."

President George W. Bush[4]

"At the dawn of the twenty-first century, the country that faced down the tyranny of fascism and communism is now called to challenge the tyranny of oil."

President Barack Obama[5]

If we have learned anything from the failed energy policies of every president since Richard Nixon, it is this: Reducing America's heavy oil import dependence is easier said than done. However, if America truly wants to return to its full potential GDP growth rate, we must significantly reduce that oil import dependence.

As a nation, we—who constitute 4.5% of the world's population and possess less than 3% of proven world oil reserves—consume almost 25% of annual world oil production. We also depend on foreign imports for 65% of our oil needs. This consumption amounts to over 20 million barrels of oil a day at a cost of almost $2 billion a day and more than $500 billion a year.[6]

Four sobering facts help define the scope of America's oil import dependence problem. First, world oil prices are not set through the free-market forces of supply and demand, but rather by a cartel—the Organization of Petroleum Exporting Countries (OPEC). To set prices, members of the OPEC cartel agree to reduce production artificially and thereby prop up the price to the desired monopoly level. In this way, they seek to extract maximum rents from buyers such as American consumers and businesses.[7]

Second, world oil demand—spurred by rapid development in China, India, and other emerging markets—is now rising at a rate faster than new oil reserves are being discovered. This growth means that oil prices are likely to be in a long-term uptrend. If nothing else changes, the pricing power of OPEC is only likely to increase.

Third, America's existing proven oil reserves are being depleted rapidly. These reserves total a little over 20 *billion* barrels of oil. Although that sounds like a lot, at our current rate of production of around 8 million barrels a day, these proven reserves will be drawn down within eight years. Moreover, even if America actually were "energy independent," with zero imports, these proven reserves would last a mere three years.

Fourth, as shown in Exhibit 7.1, most of the world's oil and natural gas reserves that America will increasingly depend on in the future are located in countries that historically have been our enemies or in countries that are prone to frequent supply disruptions because of political instability.

Exhibit 7.1   The Ten Largest Proven Oil and Gas Reserves by Country

Rank	Country	Proven Oil Reserves (in Billions of Barrels)	Rank	Country	Proven Natural Gas Reserves (in Trillions of Cubic Feet)
1	Saudi Arabia	262.3	1	Russia	1,680
2	Canada	179.21	2	Iran	971
3	Iran	136.27	3	Qatar	911
4	Iraq	115	4	Saudi Arabia	241
5	Kuwait	101.5	5	United Arab Emirates	214
6	United Arab Emirates	97.8	6	United States	193
7	Venezuela	80.012	7	Nigeria	185
8	Russia	60	8	Algeria	161
9	Libya	41.464	9	Venezuela	151
10	Nigeria	36.22	10	Iraq	112

Source: U.S. Energy Information Administration

Even a glimpse of this exhibit raises the question of whether America really wants to trust its energy future to rogue nations such as Iran, historical rivals such as Russia, erratic dictators such as Libya's Muammar Qaddafi, hothead "Cuba, sí; Yanqui, no" populists such as Venezuela's Hugo Chavez, and a civil-war-prone Nigeria plagued by frequent supply disruptions from roving gangs.

We will return to the issue of the geopolitical risks of oil import dependence. For now, however, let us simply focus on the economic dimensions.

How Does America's Oil Import Addiction Harm Our Economy? Let Us Count the Ways

To put it most simply, at a macroeconomic level, America's "addiction to oil" reduces our GDP growth rate below what it would be otherwise. America's heavy dependence on oil helps stall three of the four main drivers of our GDP Growth Drivers equation—consumption, business investment, and net exports.

Oil's brake on net exports is an obvious problem. As we noted previously, petroleum imports account for fully 40% of America's chronic trade deficits in goods.

Second, a heavy reliance on oil also helps stall our economy's consumption and investment drivers by effectively imposing a burdensome tax. For example, as oil prices rise, American consumers must pay more to fill their gas tanks to drive the same number of miles. American businesses likewise face higher production and transportation costs. The result is a loss of purchasing power for American consumers and a reduction in output and jobs for American businesses—along with downward pressure on wages and income.

As an additional growth dampener, unlike the income taxes that we pay to our government, the revenues we pay to foreign petroleum producers are not recycled into government services from which Americans can benefit. Rather, these revenues represent what economists call a "leakage" from the GDP equation. They go straight into the coffers of foreign governments, many of which do not have the United States' best interests at heart.

A third major economic problem, closely related to the first two, is that America's heavy oil import dependence makes our economy far more vulnerable to slower growth and recessions triggered by "oil price shocks." In fact, numerous economic studies have illustrated a high correlation between a rapid rise in oil prices and the onset of recession.

Regarding the broader link between oil prices and GDP growth, a study in *Applied Economics* conducted for the European Central Bank by Rebeca Jiménez-Rodríguez and Marcelo Sanchez examined the impact of oil price shocks on the major industrialized countries. The authors found that "among oil importing countries, oil price increases ... have a negative impact on economic activity in all cases but Japan."[8] Perhaps most importantly for our purposes, the observed negative GDP effects were "overall strongest for the U.S."[9]

A fourth major problem relates to the complex interactions between the value of the U.S. dollar and oil prices and the stark implications of these interactions for the conduct of U.S. monetary policy. As we discussed in Chapter 3, "Why an Easy-Money Street Is a Dead End," a strong inverse correlation exists between the value of the U.S. dollar and oil prices. As the foreign-exchange value of the dollar falls, oil prices tend to rise. As we also discussed, the value of the dollar also falls when the U.S. Federal Reserve cuts interest rates to stimulate the economy, because foreign investors are less likely to invest in the United States at the lower interest rates.

When we put together these relationships between interest rates, exchange rates, and oil prices, we come up with some very bad news for the effectiveness of monetary policy in fighting recessions. Here's the constraint:

When the Fed cuts rates to stimulate the economy, the dollar falls, and oil prices rise. Higher oil prices, in turn, reduce both consumption and business investment in the GDP Growth Driver equation, thereby at least partially offsetting any stimulative effects of lower interest rates. As the ultimate geek, physicist Sheldon on the TV show *The Big Bang Theory*, might say about this complexity and its unintended consequence, "Bazinga!"

That this problem can be significant for the American economy is evident in an analysis by Stanford economist John Taylor, to which we referred in Chapter 3. Taylor's findings are well worth repeating. In his analysis, Taylor recounts how a rate cut by the Fed triggered an oil price shock that actually helped plunge the U.S. economy deeper into recession and thereby prolonged the financial crisis:

> "When the federal funds rate was cut, oil prices broke out of the $60–$70 per barrel range and then rose rapidly throughout the first year of the financial crisis. Clearly, this bout of high oil prices hit the economy hard as gasoline prices skyrocketed and automobile sales plummeted in the spring and summer of 2008... [T]his interest-rate cut helped raise oil and other commodity prices and thereby prolonged the crisis."[10]

One very serious side effect of America's oil addiction, then, is that it limits our ability to use monetary policy as a discretionary tool to stimulate economic growth.

Risky Business

Beyond these formidable economic problems is a whole set of very significant geopolitical risks associated with America's heavy oil import dependence, as implied by the sordid cast of petroleum exporters listed in Exhibit 7.1. The biggest of these risks is the "embargo risk" associated with the possibility that one or more countries, most likely in the Persian Gulf, will cut off our oil supplies because they disagree with our foreign policy.

If you're old enough to remember the long gas lines and hard economic times of the 1973–1974 Arab oil embargo, this type of risk can still evoke a visceral anger. This embargo was triggered by U.S. military support of Israel during the Yom Kippur war; its goal was to force the United States to turn its back on Israel. It was led by Libya and Saudi Arabia. This use of the "oil weapon" was coordinated through OPEC.

More than 40 years later, geopolitical risk in the Persian Gulf continues to loom large. Although Saudi Arabia—the world's largest oil-producing nation—is now a strong U.S. ally, it continues to be vulnerable to internal pressures from Islamic extremists. In addition, Iran—the country with the second largest combined oil and gas reserves—has promised to destroy Israel. Nuclear proliferation in Iran raises the possibility of a U.S. or Israeli first strike against Iran's nuclear facilities—and likely attendant chaos in the Persian Gulf. Accordingly, the risk of another Arab oil embargo should hardly be considered minimal.

This possibility also highlights a related problem—"confrontation risk." This type of risk is associated with America's need to protect from closure key oil shipping channels such as the Persian Gulf and the Straits of Malacca. At a minimum, the existence of such risk makes the American military budget larger than it would otherwise be and the likelihood of American military intervention in the Middle East higher than it need be. A bigger defense budget is yet another subtle form of oil import tax on the American economy.

Finally, the problem of "disruption risk" also must be addressed. On almost a daily basis, world oil markets must cope with civil wars and guerrilla and criminal activity in countries such as Nigeria and the Sudan. These kinds of unrest regularly threaten the delivery of oil supplies.

*   *   *

Given the formidable economic impacts and geopolitical implications of America's heavy dependence on imported oil, it is no wonder that presidents from Nixon to Obama have called for an end to the "tyranny of oil." The obvious next question is this: What can be done?

Moving Toward Forging a Political Consensus on Reducing Oil Import Dependency

"What is sorely missing from the national dialog is any sense of urgency about America's long-term economic prospects. ... The difficult truth that must be told is that America is very close to a destructive tipping point. We must change how we conduct our politics and economics and thereby rebuild and rebalance our economy, or we will inevitably go the way of all once-great nations and suffer an irreversible decline."

This passage from this book's Introduction is useful as a prelude to any discussion of possible policy solutions to America's oil import dependence problem. It clearly identifies the urgency of the situation and the big stakes involved. Our economy is indeed at a "destructive tipping point." Only by finding a bipartisan middle ground across a wide range of issues—not the least of which is energy policy—can we avoid serious damage.

In seeking such a middle ground on energy policy, we believe there is at least one simple market-driven solution to reducing our oil import dependence that both Democrats and Republicans can find consensus on. Before offering that solution, however, we must puncture one of the most enduring and destructive myths of the American political landscape—the need for "energy independence."

In fact, "circling the wagons of autarky" is neither feasible nor desirable. Energy independence is infeasible because of the sheer scope and size of America's energy appetites. This appetite far outstrips our natural resources base and our current ability to economically conserve. Indeed, as noted earlier, America will exhaust its proven reserves in less than a decade at current production levels. In contrast, Saudi Arabia's oil reserves will last more than 70 years using the same yardstick.

Neither is total energy independence desirable, because the costs of relying simply on our own domestic energy resources and Draconian conservation measures would be far too high. Indeed, the adoption of such a strategy would render us unable to compete in today's global marketplace.

Although complete energy independence is neither feasible nor desirable, reducing our dependence on oil—and oil imports—to a level more consistent with economic prosperity and national security clearly is. Indeed, such a reduction is well within the capabilities of the country that has sent men to the moon and reigned as the world's superpower for more than 60 years. The only real question is how we should go about it. The only sensible answer is to attack the problem on both the demand and supply sides of the energy equation.

The Smart Path Embraces Both Soft- and Hard-Path Options

"We've embarked on the beginning of the last days of the age of oil.... Embrace the future and recognize the growing demand for a wide range of fuels or ignore reality and slowly—but surely—be left behind."

Mike Bowlin, Chairman and CEO of ARCO and Chairman of the American Petroleum Institute (February 1999)[11]

In attacking our oil import dependence problem, perhaps the greatest political obstacle we face is partisan gridlock. On the one hand, many Democrats prefer to solve our energy problems using "soft path" options. These range from energy conservation and regulatory fixes such as higher gas mileage standards to a greater reliance on renewables such as solar and wind. On the other hand, many Republicans prefer "hard path" options ranging from drilling for more oil and developing more domestic natural gas to the increased use of coal and nuclear power.

In fact, Democrats and Republicans are *both* right in this critical sense: The truly "smart path" to reducing our oil independence lies in embracing both hard- and soft-path options. To put this point another way, any Democrat who does not believe this country should be drilling for more oil and developing nuclear power is as foolish as any Republican who scoffs at the need for economically sensible conservation and a diversified portfolio of energy resources that includes alternatives such as wind and solar.

In fact, an important economic common denominator exists between the hard- and soft-path options. It leads us directly to at least one potentially effective market-driven policy solution to reduce our oil import dependence. That economic common denominator is captured in this "Law of Oil Import Substitution":

"As the price of oil rises, America's import dependence falls as both soft- and hard-path oil substitutes become more economically attractive."

Exhibit 7.2 shows this inverse relationship between world oil prices and U.S. oil import dependence. The percentage of oil imported by the United States is shown on the vertical axis, and the world price of a barrel of oil is shown on the horizontal axis. You can see from the downward-sloping line that as the price of oil rises, America's oil import dependence declines.

Exhibit 7.2   The Oil Import Dependence Price Curve

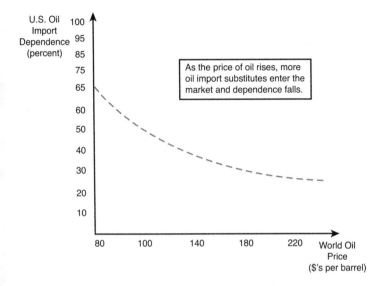

This inverse relationship exists because on the soft-path side of the oil import equation, higher oil prices cause more consumers to buy fuel-efficient cars, drive fewer miles, and retrofit their homes for energy conservation. Some businesses likewise undertake more energy conservation measures, and others switch to alternative fuels such as domestic natural gas. Still others invest in more efficient power-generating options such as cogeneration.

By the same token, on the hard-path side of the oil import equation, as oil prices rise, domestic oil producers increase their exploration and drilling activities. Difficult-to-extract oil reserves such as tar sands and shale become more and more economically feasible. As the price of oil drives up the cost of electricity, the rate of return on investments in solar and wind power likewise increases as these renewable energy sources become increasingly competitive with fossil fuel alternatives.

It is very important to note that *none of these adjustments will take place instantaneously*. Rather, Exhibit 7.2 reflects a *longer-term* adjustment process based on the well-known difference between the short- and long-run "price elasticity of demand" for oil.

The price elasticity of demand is an important economic concept that measures the responsiveness of demand to price changes. If a percentage change in price leads to a smaller percentage change in the quantity demanded, demand is said to be "inelastic." In other words, demand is not very sensitive to price changes. If the converse is true—a given percentage change in price leads to a larger percentage change in the quantity demanded—demand is said to be "elastic."

In the context of Exhibit 7.2, it is well known that in the short term, oil demand is relatively price inelastic. Thus, at least in the short term, when oil prices rise, consumers and businesses don't significantly reduce their demand. Of course, this "inelastic" demand simply reflects the difficulties of instantaneous adjustments. For example, it takes time for businesses and households to make conservation investments, and it takes more time to adopt more-costly drilling technologies.

However, over the longer term, as consumers and businesses have time to adjust both their behavior and capital stock, the price elasticity of demand for oil is greater. That's why, over time, Exhibit 7.2 provides an accurate illustration of the relationship between America's oil import dependence and world oil prices and the market-driven responses that reduce oil import consumption.

The Folly of Energy Independence Redux

The inverse relationship between world oil prices and America's oil import dependence is not the only important relationship shown in Exhibit 7.2. This exhibit also speaks directly to the economic folly of seeking complete energy independence. As you can see in the exhibit, while America's oil import dependence decreases as oil prices rise, it does so at a *decreasing* rate. This decreasing rate, which is indicated by a flattening of the oil import dependence curve as oil prices rise higher and higher, reflects one of the most ironclad laws of economics—"the law of diminishing returns."

To illustrate this law in an oil import substitution context, consider, for example, the process of extracting more oil from a given well. The easiest and cheapest oil to produce comes at the beginning of the well's life in the "primary recovery" stage, when internal pressure is high and oil gushes out. However, as a well is depleted, a producer may have to resort to more expensive "secondary recovery" techniques such as injecting water or natural gas into the well. As the well is further depleted, the driller must resort to even more expensive "tertiary recovery" techniques such as steam injection, which may not be economic at a given world oil price. This observation is reflected in the law of diminishing returns. In this case, the last barrel of oil costs a lot more to produce than the first.

It is precisely because of the law of diminishing returns that it makes absolutely no economic sense for the United States to attempt to become totally energy-independent. At some point, no matter how high the price of oil goes, it is still insufficient to prop up the economics of the alternatives. That's one big reason why America's optimal level of oil import dependence is not zero—and why the quixotic quest for "energy independence" by our presidents and politicians is totally inappropriate.

Achieving a Targeted Reduction in Oil Dependence

Exhibit 7.2 showed both the inverse relationship between oil prices and oil import dependence and the folly of pursuing complete energy independence. From these market dynamics, we may now also glean a possible policy solution that we believe is worth consideration. Exhibit 7.3 shows this two-step, market-driven solution. It involves first setting a target level of oil import dependence and then establishing a floor for the price of imported oil consistent with eliciting the soft- and hard-path responses necessary to meet that target.[12]

Exhibit 7.3   Setting a Price Floor Fee to Achieve a Target Level of Oil Import Dependence

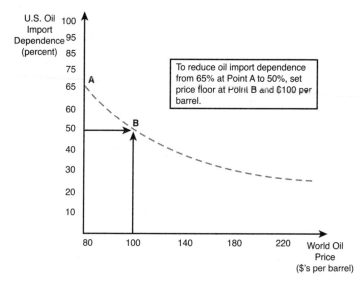

> To reduce oil import dependence from 65% at Point A to 50%, set price floor at Point B and ₵100 per barrel.

Here's how such an "oil import substitute price floor" would work. In step 1, the White House, in conjunction with the U.S. Congress and the Department of Energy, determines the desired target rate of reduction in oil use, which will reduce oil imports. This determination is based on a comprehensive cost-benefit analysis of the economic and geopolitical risks associated with different levels of oil import dependence that we identified earlier.

For example, such an analysis might yield the recommendation that the United States should cut its oil use—and reduce its import dependence—from, say, 65% to 50% over the next five years. In Exhibit 7.3, you can see that, to achieve this targeted reduction, the price of imported oil would have to be maintained at a price floor of at least $100. At this targeted price floor, enough new hard- and soft-path energy supply and demand sources would be elicited from the market over time to achieve the desired reduction in oil use and hence imports.

To achieve this targeted reduction, step 2 establishes the target price floor by imposing a *flexible* "import substitution fee" equal to the difference between the actual world price for a barrel of oil and the target price necessary to achieve the desired reduction in oil import dependence.

For example, if the world price of oil is $80 a barrel and the target $100, the initial fee is $20 a barrel. However, if the world price of oil moves up toward the target rate—say, to $90—the fee falls to $10. Moreover, whenever the world price moves above the target, *there is no fee!*

Note that such a *flexible* fee is quite different from the kind of *permanent* taxes on oil (and gasoline) that have frequently been proposed over the last three decades. Our flexible fee is very different because, to repeat, it is levied *only* when the world price of oil falls below the target level. Moreover, and again to repeat, as the world price of oil moves toward the target price, the size of the fee is reduced. Last but not least, whenever the world price of oil rises above the target level, the fee is removed, and the desired level of oil use and import reduction is achieved purely through market forces.

It is precisely this market-based flexibility and the removable nature of our proposed oil import substitute price floor fee that make it a more politically palatable solution than any permanent tax on either oil imports or gasoline—neither of which has any broad support among the general public. We also believe that any revenues raised from such a fee should be given back to the American people in the form of tax cuts—thereby making the foreign oil tax revenue-neutral.

In this regard, one temptation would be to try to use any revenues raised to support the development of alternative-energy technologies. The whole point of such a price floor, however, is that no such subsidies will be necessary to elicit the appropriate development of such technologies! The price of energy in world markets will provide sufficient motivation—so long as the appropriate threshold for the price floor fee is maintained.

The second temptation that should be resisted is to try to use any of the revenues to pay down our burgeoning budget deficits. Earmarking any such revenues in this fashion would merely feed the structural imbalance in the government expenditure element of the GDP equation and thereby harm economic growth.

As a final comment on implementation, should the target price of the desired oil import reduction be significantly above the current price of oil when the policy is implemented, any oil import substitute fee should be phased in to minimize any possible short-term disruption to the economy.

Why This Proposal Has Economic and Political Merit

In proposing this solution, we believe that Democrats can embrace such an approach because it fulfills the goals of promoting energy conservation and environmental stewardship and developing alternative-energy sources. These goals would not be economically feasible when world oil prices are below the targeted threshold. The flexible nature of the fee likewise reduces concerns about the regressivity of such a tax and any transient negative impacts on the poor.

We also believe that Republicans can embrace such a proposal because it is market-driven, it is revenue-neutral, and it is applied only when the price of oil rises above the target. Moreover, this simple market-driven mechanism removes the need for any elaborate regulatory programs such as fuel efficiency standards for cars—which likewise should have great appeal to Republicans. Our approach also eliminates the need to heavily subsidize any one of a number of import substitutes, whether corn-based ethanol, coal-to-liquid synfuels, or renewables.

As a final observation in support of this policy solution, we also note that our approach solves one of the most vexing problems plaguing energy conservation efforts—particularly, the development of renewable energy: the historical boom-and-bust cycle of oil prices. Here's the problem:

When oil prices are booming, consumers rush to buy fuel-efficient cars, and alternative-energy producers find it more and more economic to get solar and wind projects online. However, once oil prices go bust, the legs of these alternative-energy substitutes are cut out from beneath them.

From a national investment perspective, the boom-and-bust oil price cycle and its attendant volatility significantly raise the risk of investments in oil import substitution technologies over a wide range of options. This higher risk, in turn, is reflected in a higher cost of capital for these projects and a lower rate of development—and therefore less oil import substitution.

Our proposal for a flexible and removable price floor solves this problem of volatility by insuring market participants against the downside of periodic oil price busts. This floor will lower the risk, and therefore the cost of capital investment, in such projects for all market participants.

We believe such a price floor strategy is all the more important because the OPEC cartel understands that one of the best ways it can preserve its pricing power is to periodically allow oil prices to fall to make oil substitutes uneconomic and more risky.

The Thorny Politics of Oil Import Fees

Of course, we understand that the politics of any such proposed oil import fee are difficult at best. After all, nobody likes a new fee or tax. However, in the context of America's oil import dependence, it is well worth considering a flexible, removable, and revenue-neutral price floor fee on every barrel of imported oil sold at a price below the target. Such a policy would help us avoid both the heavy hand of regulation and any permanent taxes on oil or gasoline.

Our market-driven approach likewise would help us avoid wasteful government programs like that established by the Obama administration to promote the creation of so-called "green jobs." At a cost of $136,000 per job, this type of program is hardly a bargain in today's economy.

Our approach is also fully consistent with economic theory and the existence of what economists call "negative externalities." In the context of America's oil import dependence, the world market price of oil clearly does not fully reflect the high economic costs and geopolitical risks that our oil import dependence imposes on our country. In such a case, it is economically efficient to "internalize" the negative externality by charging an appropriate fee. This fee would be equal to the difference between the private cost of oil to individual market participants and the social costs to the broader country imposed by the existence of significant economic and geopolitical risks.

*   *   *

In closing, we would like to say that we are in no way "Club of Rome" or Malthusian pessimists on America's energy future. We fully believe that in the presence of appropriate market signals, our energy economy has the resources, technologies, and innovative creativity to significantly reduce our oil import dependence over time. We can do so in a way that helps, rather than harms, our economy, and in a way that poses no undue sacrifice to our standard of living.

We also understand that a comprehensive U.S. energy policy is more complicated than any single fee on oil to reduce our dependence. For example, in order for nuclear power to once again be viable, we need more standardized reactor designs and a more elegant solution to waste disposal. Similarly, our existing "food to fuel" ethanol program needs a very serious debate about whether this program really provides any net benefit or is simply a special-interest boondoggle. Thorny environmental issues are associated with more oil drilling—particularly in the aftermath of the 2010 BP oil spill in the Gulf of Mexico—or the placement of more wind farms or large-scale solar facilities.

We understand these complications and complexities, but their debate is beyond the scope of this book. What we are focusing on with our message is how to restore America's economy to its full potential GDP growth rate using the insights gleaned from our Ten Levers of Growth and GDP Growth Drivers analyses. In the spirit of Occam's Razor, we have offered what we believe would be a very simple but important step toward solving a problem long in need of attention and solution.

THERE'S NO FREE ENERGY AND NO FREE LUNCH

We live in a world of trade-offs in which all energy resources have their downsides. This chapter has discussed the numerous economic and geopolitical risks of using oil. In a similar vein, coal is dangerous to mine and pollutes the air. Nuclear power runs the risk of a core meltdown such as Three Mile Island, raises formidable waste-disposal problems, and opens the door to nuclear proliferation. Wind energy requires vast amounts of land, lacks a high degree of reliability, is noisy, and slaughters thousands of birds every year. Solar power is cheap to produce once the solar panels are put in place, but the manufacture of solar panels is both expensive and energy-intensive. Even energy conservation has its downsides. For example, a well insulated building often creates air-quality issues because stagnant air builds up. Of course, some of these risks are more compelling than others. A nuclear core meltdown certainly trumps noise issues with wind power. However, the broader point is that no energy technology is without its disadvantages. We need to depend in some degree on every energy technology if we are to overcome our oil import dependency problem.

Thus, if we truly want to reduce our oil import dependence using the power of market forces—rather than a heavy regulatory hand—one of the best ways to do so is to ensure that the price of oil remains above a certain target level associated with our target level of oil import dependence.

Endnotes

1. State of the Union address, President Richard Nixon, January 30, 1974.

2. President Gerald R. Ford's address before a joint session of Congress, reporting on the state of the Union, January 15, 1975.

3. Speech to the nation, "Energy and the National Goals: A Crisis of Confidence," July 15, 1979.

4. State of the Union address, President George W. Bush, January 31, 2006.

5. Remarks of Senator Barack Obama to the Detroit Economic Club, May 20, 2007.

6. This calculation conservatively assumes a price of $80 per barrel of oil.

7. OPEC had difficulty enforcing price discipline earlier in its history because of cheating by its members. For example, countries such as Libya and Iran would pump more oil than their quota. However, OPEC has grown increasingly powerful as the world market for oil has tightened.

8. Rebeca Jiménez-Rodríguez and Marcelo Sanchez. "Oil Price Shocks and Real GDP Growth: Empirical Evidence for Some OECD Countries." *Applied Economics*, 2005(37): 201–228.

9. Ibid, p. 203.

10. John B. Taylor. *Getting Off Track*. Stanford, California: Hoover Institution Press, 2009.

11. Bowlin is now with BP. This speech was delivered in Houston on February 9, 1999.

12. A similar approach is set forth in "The Petroleum-Tax Giveback: A Commentary by Thomas W. Merrill and David M. Schizer." *Commentary*, October 2009.

PART IV

Good Politics Usually Makes for Bad Economics

Why has reforming Medicare, Medicaid, and Social Security been so difficult? And why is undertaking such reforms so extremely important to the long-term health of the American economy? How has the passage of ObamaCare legislation set up both our health care system and our broader economy for failure? And should we try to fix ObamaCare or simply start over? The next two chapters tackle these critical questions.

Chapter 8, "Cutting the Gordian Knot of Entitlements," explains why, in the absence of reform, the rapidly escalating funding requirements of Social Security, Medicare, and Medicaid will inexorably lead to a massive tax burden, a massive debt burden, or the squeezing out of virtually every other expenditure in the U.S. federal budget. In each scenario, our economy is doomed to performing well below its potential as higher taxes, higher interest rates, or runaway inflation slam on the brakes. To avoid this fate, we introduce a comprehensive plan to save Social Security. However, we caution that, because of rapidly rising health care costs, it will be far harder to make Medicare and Medicaid whole than to rescue Social Security.

Chapter 9, "Why ObamaCare Makes Our Economy Sick," illustrates that President Barack Obama was right to pursue health care reform, but wrong to pass the legislation he did. Rather than address the most important problem facing our health care system—out-of-control costs—ObamaCare represents yet another inadequately funded entitlement program that will both weaken our health care system and put another brake on our long-term growth potential. We recommend starting over. Thus, we describe three market-driven policy changes that would do a far better job of achieving the objectives of lower-cost and higher-quality care.

chapter eight

Cutting the Gordian Knot of Entitlements

"If I tell you how things are, I have told you why things cannot change."

Edward Banfield (1916–1999)

This classic assessment of the difficult politics of change from one of Harvard's most notable political scientists aptly describes the inability of the American political system to come to grips with one of the greatest threats to our long-term prosperity. This threat is the explosive growth of three entitlement programs that together already consume over 40% of the entire federal budget—Social Security, Medicare, and Medicaid.

Let us make no mistake about this. Unless we change the current policy trajectory, decades—not just days—of reckoning will occur as ballooning expenditures on these programs take an ever-larger bite out of our GDP and ability to grow.

In fact, the Congressional Budget Office (CBO) estimates that Social Security expenditures will rise from 4.3% of our GDP to 6% by 2033.[1] For Medicare and Medicaid, the trend is even more alarming. If the rise in health care costs continues to dramatically outpace the rise in economic growth, Medicare and Medicaid obligations will escalate from a little more than 4% of GDP today to 13% by 2035— and 22% by 2080.[2]

From the perspective of the GDP Growth Drivers equation, these are truly astonishing numbers. Historically, the *entire* federal budget has averaged about 20% of GDP a year over the past 30 years. However, unless these entitlement programs are brought under control, Social Security, Medicare, and Medicaid *alone* may eventually consume over 20% of GDP.

Absent reform, the rapidly escalating funding requirements of America's triple entitlement threat will inexorably lead to either a massive tax burden, a massive debt burden, or the squeezing out of virtually every other expenditure in the U.S. federal budget. In all three of these dismal "entitlement financing" scenarios, our economy will be doomed to performing well below its potential as higher taxes, higher interest rates, or runaway inflation slam on the brakes.

Despite this looming crisis—and despite a steady parade of Congressional reports, task forces, think-tank treatises, and partisan polemics—our politicians continue to expand America's entitlement programs rather than rein them in. Consider the fiscally irresponsible behavior of just our past two presidents—and the Congresses that served them.

In 2003, with bipartisan support, President George W. Bush pushed through a massive Medicare prescription drug benefit. The right-of-center American Enterprise Institute described it as "the most fiscally irresponsible legislation in U.S. history."[3] The left-of-center Brookings Institution predicted that it would "indisputably and significantly deepen an already horrendous fiscal mess."[4] Mr. Bush's woefully underfunded new entitlement alone will add more than half a trillion dollars in expenditures just by 2015 and another $1.5 to $2 trillion in the succeeding decade to a program already facing severe financial stress. And the new entitlement did little to restrain costs.

In similar fashion, in March 2010, with the help of a Congressional Democratic majority (and some parliamentary sleight of hand),

President Barack Obama passed a health care plan that will add an estimated 16 million Americans to Medicaid—and another half-trillion dollars to America's budget deficits just in its first ten years. Just like former President Bush, President Obama did so without credibly addressing *the* most important issue in health care for our economic future: cost containment.

As to why entitlement "reform" continues to move in exactly the wrong, budget-busting direction, we borrow from the words of Professor Banfield from the beginning of this chapter to describe "how things are":

- Politicians from the White House to Capitol Hill seeking reelection are as eager to create new entitlement programs and benefits as they are loath to find ways to pay for them.
- Retirees receiving entitlement benefits vote in far greater numbers than the younger members of the workforce contributing to the financing of the entitlement programs.
- Liberal think tanks and lobbying groups for seniors immediately jump on any attempts at reform.
- Hence, benefits are never reduced—and often are increased. We fiddle while our budget burns.

The Imperative of an Economic Rather Than Accounting Solution

"Today's young workers and children are about to be engulfed by a massive income transfer from young to old that will perversely make it harder for them to care for their own children."

Robert Samuelson

In thinking about how to finally cut the Gordian knot of entitlement reform—and break the Banfield stalemate—it's useful to begin with this cautionary note: Far too often, within the mountain of books, reports, and newspaper articles on the subject, entitlement reform is approached not as a complex and dynamic economic process but rather as a simple accounting exercise. From this "bean counter's" perspective, all politicians need to do to solve the crisis is have the political courage to raise taxes and cut benefits. Often lost in this translation is the overriding need to ensure that our economy performs at its full potential GDP growth rate.

Any entitlement reform package must allow our economy to perform at its full potential for two reasons. First, strong economic growth will generate the maximum possible income and tax revenues to help pay for these entitlement programs. Second, strong economic growth will minimize the strains elsewhere on the federal budget by reducing the need for social welfare payments for the unemployed—who instead will have more, and higher-paying, job opportunities.

Because of the accounting orientation and tax hike focus of much of the entitlement reform analysis, our value added in this debate will be to run America's looming entitlement crisis through the filters of our GDP Growth Drivers equation and the Ten Levers of Growth. In doing so, we will thereby illustrate this Iron Law of Entitlement Reform:

> Any attempt to close the looming entitlement spending gap by (further) raising taxes, running large budget deficits, or cutting spending on critical needs such as education and infrastructure will backfire and result in less innovation and entrepreneurship, slower economic growth, lower wages, fewer people employed, less tax revenue collected, and an even larger budget deficit gap.

Why Social Security Is Easier to Fix Than Medicare and Medicaid

Before we begin our analysis of each of the three major U.S. entitlement programs, it's useful to make this big-picture observation: It will be much easier to make Social Security whole than it will be to address the wreckage that is now Medicare and Medicaid. Why? Social Security expenditures are increasing primarily for one reason—an aging population.

In contrast, expenditures on Medicare and Medicaid are increasing for two reasons: an aging population *and* a rate of growth in health care costs that is far exceeding the rate of growth in per capita GDP. In fact, the much bigger cost driver of Medicare and Medicaid is rapidly rising health care costs—not population growth. Indeed, since the 1970s, health care costs have grown at a rate fully 2.9 percentage points faster than has per capita GDP.

Exhibit 8.1 illustrates how the "excess growth costs" of health care are likely to drive up total federal spending on Medicare and Medicaid. With the percentage of GDP on the vertical axis, this CBO chart is straight out of a horror novel. You can see that if excess costs continue to rise by their historical rate of 2.5%—a likely scenario under current policy—Medicare and Medicaid expenditures soar past 20% of GDP by 2050.

We will discuss this issue of rising health care costs much more in the next chapter. For now, this exhibit should serve as stark testimony to the fact that the passage of "health care reform" in March 2010 planted yet another seed of economic destruction. As we have noted, this new legislation did virtually nothing to address the rising costs illustrated in Exhibit 8.1. At the same time, it added a new, massive, and severely underfunded entitlement program to the American political and economic landscape.

Exhibit 8.1 Total Federal Spending for Medicare and Medicaid

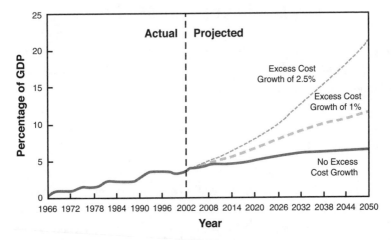

Source: CBO, Long Term Budget Outlook 2009

Saving Social Security in Two Easy Pieces

"In net present value terms, Social Security owes $6.8 trillion dollars more in benefits than it will receive in taxes."

2007 Social Security Trustees Report

Social Security is the largest government program in the world and the single biggest expense item in the federal budget. Currently, over 50 million Americans annually receive more than $600 billion in retirement benefits, while 162 million workers are paying payroll taxes to support the program.

In thinking about how to reform Social Security without damaging both our economy and society, you really need to know only five things about its origins, structure, and evolution. First, when Social

Security was established in 1935 by President Franklin Roosevelt, the retirement age was set at roughly the same age as the life expectancy of the average working American—65. This tight correspondence between eligibility and life expectancy meant, from the outset, that the program's effective payouts would be relatively small.

Of course, since then, average life expectancy has risen to close to 80, while the eligibility age has only risen to 67 (but only for citizens born after 1959).[5] This ever-increasing mismatch between benefit eligibility and life expectancy has been a surefire recipe for rapidly rising program liabilities.

Second, Social Security was never intended to be the sole source of income for American retirees, but rather a supplemental source. However, millions of Americans have come to depend largely on Social Security along with Medicare as their "retirement package." This dependence has had the perverse effect of discouraging individual savings and investment in private retirement programs and the broader economy.

Third—and this has proven to be the demographic Achilles' heel of the entire system—Social Security was *not* set up as a true pension fund, whereby contributions are collected and then invested to fund future payouts. Rather, it was set up as a "pay-as-you-go" system in which current workers provide the contributions to finance the benefits of current retirees.

When Social Security started paying old-age benefits in 1940, this "pay-as-you-go" system worked fine. There were almost 50 workers to support every retiree.[6] By 1950, the worker-to-retiree ratio was still a very robust 16 to 1, even as more and more retirees were added to the benefit rolls and life expectancy began to climb significantly.[7]

Today, however, as our population has aged, the worker-to-retiree ratio has shrunk to around three workers for every retiree. By the year

2050, the ratio will dip to close to two.[8] This growing mismatch between available workers to fund the program and the growing number of retirees has become a recipe for the mother of all intergenerational conflicts. Current younger workers and their children face a bleak future of massive obligations.

Fourth, because of this growing mismatch between workers and retirees working in combination with the slow economic growth of the 2000s, *the Social Security Administration has already begun paying out more in benefits than it is taking in from payroll taxes!* Although this crossing of the "negative cash flow Rubicon" for Social Security was inevitable, it was still a stunning turn of events, because it arrived fully six years sooner than the CBO had forecast.

The CBO forecast was wrong for two reasons. Double-digit unemployment during the Great Recession of 2007 2009 significantly reduced the amount of payroll taxes collected. These bad times also encouraged many seniors to take early retirement at 62, effectively turning Social Security into a form of unemployment compensation as well as a pension.

That the CBO forecast was wrong for these two reasons underscores the central theme of this book: If we are to deal with all the economic problems bearing down on us without engaging in the economic suicide of massive tax hikes or out-of-control budget deficits, it is critical that the American economy grow robustly at its full potential GDP growth rate.

The fifth and final thing we all need to know about Social Security is that once it goes into a negative cash flow position, as it now has, it is supposed to begin drawing down on the alleged Social Security "trust fund" surpluses. These alleged surpluses supposedly were built up over the years during which we had plenty of workers to support retirees and payroll tax contributions exceeded benefit payments.

These alleged trust fund surpluses are supposed to last us until at least 2037—at which point the system officially goes broke.

That we can rely on these alleged trust funds to fund Social Security, at least for a few more decades, is, of course, just hocus-pocus. America's alleged Social Security surpluses are more a budgetary mirage than an actual pot of money at the end of any bureaucratic rainbow.

These surpluses largely exist in the form of paper "IOUs" that the government issued to itself so that it can pay for other deficit expenditures in the federal budget. To put this shell game another way, our free-spending government has come to depend on the Social Security surpluses over the years to make its balance sheet and budget deficits look "less worse" than they actually are.

This fiscally irresponsible charade is captured in the concept of the "unified budget," which credits the surpluses that exist in "off-budget" items such as Social Security to the main federal budget. As long as Social Security ran a surplus, this charade had the effect of making the budget deficits look smaller than they actually were. Now, with Social Security in the negative cash flow position, the charade is over.

In summary, these five features of the Social Security program virtually ensure a crisis:

- A growing gap between the retirement age and life expectancy
- Perverse incentives against savings and investment
- A pay-as-you-go system characterized by a steady fall in the number of workers who can support a growing number of retirees
- Social Security crossing the negative cash flow Rubicon in 2010

- The past use of surplus Social Security funds to finance other federal budget expenditures so that no "trust funds" actually exist

Closing the Social Security Spending Gap: What *Won't* Work

Exhibit 8.2, taken from the annual Social Security Trustees Report, conservatively illustrates the growing gap between Social Security spending and the tax revenues being taken in to support the program. We say "conservatively" because the Trustees Report has consistently underforecast the problems looming with Social Security.[9]

Exhibit 8.2   Social Security Benefits and Tax Revenues as a Percentage of GDP

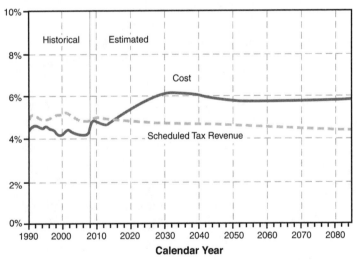

In theory, there are numerous possible ways to close what will be the growing gap between revenues and expenditures in our Social Security system. In practice, however, only a few of these ways pass our GDP Growth Drivers equation and Ten Levers of Growth test. Let's first rule out what won't work.

The first nonoption, which is always first on the list of the "accountant reformers," is to further raise the payroll tax. One option is to do so directly by raising the payroll tax rate from its current level of 6.2% on both employees and employers. Another option is to do so indirectly via a "Robin Hood" raising of the so-called "wage cap." Right now, workers pay into the system on wages up to $106,800. Proposals range from lifting the cap by thousands of dollars to eliminating the cap.

From the perspective of the GDP Growth Drivers equation, this "solution" is destructive. Higher taxes on individuals would reduce work effort consumption in the growth equation. Higher taxes on businesses would reduce investment, along with all the jobs, innovation, and wage growth that come with such investment. Using a "tax the rich" strategy by raising the wage cap would be equally counterproductive, because the burden of any such tax would fall primarily on middle-income workers and small businesses—the two most reliable engines of economic growth.

A second nonoption is to cut government spending on other discretionary programs to make way for the entitlement programs. The problem is that the spending gap is so large that we would have to eliminate virtually the entire budget for defense, education, highways, and our criminal justice system—and we would still be unable to close the gap. Obviously, this approach is a nonstarter.

A third nonoption is to simply run ever-larger budget deficits and finance these deficits through the sale of bonds. However, as the government issues more and more bonds, eventually it will have to offer higher and higher interest rates to consummate the sale of the bonds. Of course, higher interest rates will depress both critically needed business investment and "big-ticket item" consumption in the GDP Growth Drivers equation, thereby slowing economic growth.

This crowding out of consumption and investment in the GDP Growth Drivers equation is not the only problem with running up more and more government bond debt. Economic and geopolitical effects also result from owing more and more of our debt to foreigners.

Since 1970, the percent of debt held by foreigners has risen from about 4% to almost 40%—and it continues to rise. From an economic growth point of view, the ever-increasing interest payments on the debt that we "export" to the rest of the world represent a significant, growth-stalling leakage of purchasing power from the domestic economy.

America's geopolitical problem has to do with the fact that more and more of our foreign debt is being held by countries that may seek to use political leverage as a major creditor. In fact, we saw the power of such leverage during the 2007–2009 financial crisis.

During that crisis, both Japan and China exerted significant pressure on the U.S. government to guarantee the debt of Fannie Mae and Freddie Mac. These two countries held in combination hundreds of billions of dollars in financial instruments issued by these government-sponsored mortgage-issuing entities. This foreign-government pressure was indeed successful, as the U.S. government responded by guaranteeing $5 trillion of that debt.

Closing the Social Security Spending Gap: What *Can* Work

"If no substantial action is taken until the combined trust funds become exhausted in 2037, then changes necessary to make Social Security solvent over the next 75 years will be concentrated on fewer years and fewer cohorts.... The projected trust fund deficits should be addressed in a timely way to allow for a gradual phasing in of the necessary changes and to provide advance notice to workers. Making adjustments sooner will allow them to be spread over more generations."

2009 Social Security Trustees Report[10]

If higher taxes, cutting other government spending, or running ever-larger budget deficits will not solve our Social Security problem, just what *will* work? We believe that two options, working in combination, have the potential to close all, or almost all, of the forecast spending gap: raising the retirement age to match rising life expectancy better, and indexing initial benefits to prices rather than wages so as to maintain real, inflation-adjusted purchasing power for beneficiaries.

Raising the Retirement Age: An Idea Whose Time Has (Finally) Come?

Raising the retirement age is hardly a new idea. Scores of bills have been introduced in Congress over the last several decades seeking to do just that—thus far with only one modest adjustment (to age 67 for people born after 1959). This pattern of failure notwithstanding, two things have changed.

First, with Social Security now paying out more in benefits than it collects in taxes, years before expected, the crisis has abruptly reached a tipping point—and it will only worsen with time. Second, the U.S. government is already facing historically massive budget deficits—even without a big deficit in Social Security. These deficits have helped further raise public awareness about both the dangers of running large deficits and the limits of our ability to further tax our way out of the budget crisis.

Within the context of these two harsh realities, public opinion—and therefore the political process—should be more receptive to raising the retirement age. The caveat is that this must be done in a gradual and orderly fashion. If done in such a way, this political middle-ground approach would go a long way toward relieving the Social Security burden. It would go even further toward restoring some semblance of intergenerational equity between the increasing number of retirees and the younger workers being asked to support them.

To see how such a reform might be implemented, consider this three-step illustrative proposal based on the CBO's Long-Term Budget Outlook:[11]

1. Immediately raise the retirement age to 67 for anyone born after 1954 (instead of 1959).

2. Thereafter, raise the retirement age by two months per year until it reaches age 70.

3. After that, raise the retirement age by one month every other year to reflect rising life-expectancy rates.

The obvious political advantage of this gradualist option is that it does not place an undue burden on those who are currently near Social Security retirement. According to a CBO study, taking such a step would cut Social Security's share of the GDP by almost a full percentage point and save about 12% by the year 2050.[12]

The merits of this proposal notwithstanding, the following passage from a Congressional Research Service report for Congress accurately summarizes the counterarguments:

"Opponents of raising the retirement age say that it is simply a cut in benefits, which would unfairly penalize workers who planned their retirement based on current law. They aver that the burden would be concentrated on those unable to work until later ages because they are unemployed or work in arduous occupations. They maintain it would adversely affect those racial minorities that have relatively shorter life spans. They dispute that increased longevity necessarily corresponds with ability to work at later ages—people may be living longer, but with more chronic illnesses and impairments."[13]

Although we are sympathetic to these arguments, taken as a group they still do not trump the logic of better matching benefit payouts with rising life expectancies, restoring intergenerational equity across our generations, and making Social Security whole without doing any long-term economic damage.

Price-Indexing Initial Benefits: The Ultimate Bridge to Intergenerational Equity

"Currently, initial [Social Security] benefits are set by a complex formula that calculates workers' average annual earnings in their 35 highest-paid years and adjusts those earnings up from those years to reflect standards of living near that worker's retirement age. That adjustment is based on wage growth over that time span. Under the commission plan, the adjustment would be based instead on the rise of consumer prices.

"The change would save trillions of dollars in scheduled expenditures and solve Social Security's long-term deficit...."

Washington Post (January 2005)[14]

This excerpt accurately explains both the mechanics and budget implications of an innovative proposal offered up by the 2005 Commission to Strengthen Social Security. As noted in the *Washington Post*, Social Security benefits are now set by indexing those initial benefits to wage inflation.

Because wages have historically risen significantly faster than prices, this wage indexing amounts to an extra boost in purchasing power for retirees. The problem, of course, is that this boost has not been properly funded by the payroll taxes that retirees and their employers have made into the system.

To understand the intergenerational redistributive implications of this unfunded boost in benefits, consider these words from Harvard economist Gregory Mankiw during his tenure as Chairman of the Council of Economic Advisers for the George W. Bush White House:

> "[U]nder current law, each generation of retirees receives higher real benefits than the generation before it. This stems from the indexation of the initial level of benefits to wages, which over time grow faster than prices. A person with average wages retiring at age 65 this year gets an annual benefit of about $14,000, but a similar person retiring in 2050 is scheduled to get over $20,000 in today's dollars. In other words, even after adjusting for inflation, a typical person's benefits are scheduled to rise by over 40 percent."[15]

It is precisely because of this large wage indexing skew that a far more equitable and fiscally responsible alternative is price indexing. The beauty of this alternative is that it does not result in any loss of real purchasing power by beneficiaries. Instead, by the very definition of price indexing, benefits keep pace with the rate of inflation. In this way, retirees' real purchasing power and standard of living are preserved.

Of course, because benefits are lower under price indexing than wage indexing, opponents of this reform have described it as a benefit "cut." That may well be true under a loose definition of a "cut," but price indexing does not, to repeat, cut retirees' real purchasing power.

Price indexing preserves real purchasing power while generating substantial cost savings. Therefore, not only is it arguably a more equitable alternative to the current system, but it also is the single most powerful policy we could adopt to effectively close the Social Security spending gap.

In fact, as the CBO has noted, price indexing alone would lower Social Security's share of the GDP to 4.7% from that which is projected for 2050—the previously noted 6.4%. In doing so, price indexing would close over 70% of the projected 75-year Social Security shortfall.[16]

Forging a Political Consensus

Here, then, is the big picture: The combination of raising the retirement age and moving to a price-indexing system would close all, or almost all, of the future Social Security spending gap we now face. This set of reforms would do so with the least damage to our economy and in a way that would guarantee greater intergenerational equity and thereby minimize future political conflict. The only remaining question is whether a political consensus can be forged over this reform package.

One point is key to the formation of any such political consensus. The Social Security coalition of liberal think tanks and senior groups must realize that this reform package offers the best hope of saving one of the most important programs in American society. To ensure support from this coalition, two additional issues must be considered.

The first has to do with the phase-in time for price indexing. As with raising the retirement age, we recommend a gradual, rather than abrupt, transition over the next decade. That way, individuals very near retirement, with insufficient time to adapt, are not unduly burdened.

The second issue has to do with how the burden of price indexing falls on lower- versus higher-income recipients. One way to handle this issue in equity is to adopt a progressive system of indexing such as was also proposed by the 2005 Commission to Strengthen Social Security. Under a progressive indexing system, low-income beneficiaries would continue to receive their Social Security benefits using the wage-indexing formula. Benefits for middle- and higher-income retirees would be calculated using price indexing. We believe this is an idea worth exploring, because it would help preserve the most important function of Social Security—being a safety net for seniors.

As a final point in support of the move to price-indexing initial benefits, this would actually represent a return to original policy. As Gregory Mankiw argued the case in 2005:

> "This current system of indexing initial benefits to wages has not been part of Social Security since its inception. In fact, it was introduced by the Carter administration in 1977. At that time, some leading experts on Social Security objected to this change, arguing that it would put Social Security on an unsustainable path. In a prescient letter to the *New York Times* (published on May 29, 1977), Peter Diamond, James Heckman, William Hsiao, and Ernest Moorehead wrote, 'the wage indexing method calls for a much larger growth in benefits for future retirement age at a time when the country may not be able to afford it.'"[17]

We can't say we weren't warned—but it is not too late to return to where the system started. The sidebar at the end of this chapter describes the path to do so.

Saving Medicare and Medicaid: Mission Impossible?

As bad as our Social Security crisis is, our Medicare and Medicaid crisis is far worse. This is because, as we noted previously, the primary cost driver for Medicare and Medicaid is not an aging population but rather out-of-control health care costs. Several critical points follow from this observation:

- One of the best options available for saving Social Security—raising the age of eligibility to better match rising life expectancies—provides only a small step toward resolving our Medicare/Medicaid crisis.

- The only way to stop Medicare and Medicaid from devouring an ever-larger share of America's economic pie is to bring health care costs under control.

- We could also make progress by focusing Medicare and Medicaid spending more on lower-income households.

Regrettably, the last two bullet points have not been the focus of reforms. Instead, as discussed in the next chapter, President Obama's Patient Protection and Affordable Care Act (aka "ObamaCare") simply and dramatically expands both Medicare and Medicaid spending while doing little to address the cost-containment issue.

Indeed, by the end of the decade, ObamaCare will have added some 16 million Americans to Medicaid as part of its insurance coverage mandate. It will also provide hundreds of billions of dollars more in prescription drug benefits for Medicare recipients.

In effect, then, all ObamaCare has done is create a very large new entitlement program. Part of it remains an unfunded liability, and another part will be funded by growth-stalling tax hikes and penalty fees. In this way, President Obama has violated one of this book's central tenets: One of the best ways to ensure that sufficient funds exist for our national priorities and for reducing our budget deficits is to ensure that we grow at our maximum potential GDP growth rate of more than 3% annually. This goal is precisely why we must avoid any "reforms" such as further tax hikes that push us in the opposite direction.

A Flexible and Focused Way Forward

Although ObamaCare is clearly not the answer, there is a path forward to reducing the drain of Medicare and Medicaid spending on our national prosperity. This reform can be done to maintain these programs' ability to serve as a safety net for lower-income Americans. However, the changes will require flexibility and focus as well as greater cost-consciousness.

For Medicaid, flexibility is the key. Unlike the federally run Medicare, Medicaid is a joint federal-state program. Although each state runs its own system, it must conform to fairly rigid federal guidelines to receive matching funds and grants.[18]

A more flexible approach means moving to a block grant type of structure of federal support. The federal government would annually give each state the Medicaid funding it received the year before, adjusted for inflation and for changes in the state's population of low-income individuals—with few or no strings attached. With this block grant structure, each state could fashion its Medicaid health care program as it so chose—with traditional Medicaid, supporting private insurance, funding community health centers, and so on. In fact, there would be much to learn about cost containment and much to gain by fostering such state-level innovation.

For Medicare, the watchwords are cost-consciousness and focus. The cost-conscious approach here is to set an explicit annual budget for Medicare. This would be a much preferred alternative to our now "mandatory" spending frame of mind, which is simply inconsistent with the productivity enhancements and cost control we need.

To focus Medicare, we must also move away from the current fee-for-service reimbursement system. Instead, Medicare could give each retiree support for a basic health plan, which individuals could supplement at their own expense. Support should focus on lower-income individuals, with much less assistance for more affluent seniors.

Although they aren't as easy as the Social Security fix, flexibility and focus together with more cost-consciousness can address our health care budget woes—if we have the courage to reform health care in a patient-friendly and market-driven way. Ultimately, however, we will never be able to "fix" either Medicare or Medicaid unless we bring health care costs under control. That topic is the subject of the next chapter.

What About Social Security "Personal Accounts"?

In 2005, the Bush administration had a significant window of opportunity to bring about a constructive compromise on Social Security reform. However, that window slammed shut largely because of President Bush's fixation on including so-called "personal accounts" as part of any revamping of Social Security.

Although many economists (including one of us) have supported personal accounts as a better way to prefinance Social Security benefits, personal accounts on their own do not offer higher, risk-adjusted returns. Therefore, they do not solve the biggest problem facing Social Security—the looming spending gap.

Although President Bush understood this, his primary emphasis on personal accounts during the debate sent the wrong message. In fact, many Democrats saw personal accounts as the thin end of the wedge to dismantle traditional Social Security—and therefore recused themselves from any possible compromise.

At the time, President Bush should have just jettisoned the term "personal accounts" and offered add-on expanded saving incentives. For example, he could have proposed letting individuals contribute more pretax dollars to IRAs and other preexisting savings vehicles.

As part of any compromise, President Bush also could have focused on low-income workers, because Social Security's central role was to be a safety net for seniors. He could have done this by supporting higher benefits for low-income workers than their record of contributions might offer, or by matching the contributions to private savings incentives with refundable tax credits.

To pay for these changes and restore Social Security's long-term financial stability, Congress could have slowed the growth rate of benefits for middle- and upper-income workers. Such a compromise would have achieved the goals of increasing private saving for retirement insurance and shoring up Social Security's ability to meet the retirement needs of millions of Americans. Yet Mr. Bush's overemphasis on personal accounts allowed opponents to exploit inconsistencies in his reform agenda.

As we will discuss in the next chapter, President Obama has made a similar mistake in his crusade for health care. Rather than focusing on cost control, which is the central problem facing the system, he has chosen to focus primarily on universal coverage and a stealth "public option." Even though Mr. Obama passed his health care bill, he failed to reach any broad public consensus on the legislation. That failure to reach a public consensus—along with its ominous fiscal implications—will eventually be ObamaCare's undoing.

Endnotes

1. Congressional Budget Office. "Long-Term Projections for Social Security: 2009 Update," p. 2. August 2009.

2. Congressional Budget Office. "The Long Term Budget Outlook, 2009," p. 21. Total spending for Medicare and Medicaid has risen from 1.7% of GDP in fiscal year 1975 to 5.7% in fiscal year 2008. Over the same period, net federal spending for the two programs rose from 1.2% of GDP to 4.1%. CBO projects that without significant changes in policy, total spending for health care will be 31% of GDP by 2035 and will increase to 46% by 2080. Total spending for Medicare is projected to increase to 8% of GDP by 2035 and to 15% by 2080. Total spending for Medicaid is projected to increase to 5% of GDP by 2035 and to 7% by 2080.

3. Joseph Antos and Jagadeesh Gokhale. "The Medicare Prescription-Drug Benefit Is Bad for America's Health." AEI Online. June 26, 2003.

4. Henry J. Aaron, Senior Fellow, Economic Studies. "Prescription Drug Bill: The Good, the Bad, and the Ugly. Health Care, Medicare, U.S. Economy, Washington, DC." http://www.brookings.edu/articles/2004/0115useconomics_aaron.aspx.

5. Recipients can retire as early as 62, but benefits are reduced.

6. William R. Larsen. "Worker-to-Retiree Ratio." October 10, 2002. http://www.justsayno.50megs.com/wr_ratio.html.

7. Michael Tanner. "Social Security: Follow the Math." January 14, 2005. http://www.socialsecurity.org/pubs/articles/tanner-050114.html.

8. Ibid.

9. This problem manifests itself in the need for the Trustees Report to move up both the year in which Social Security is forecast to go broke and the year in which it will have cash flow.

10. The official name of this report is the 2009 OASDI Trustees Report, where OASDI stands for Old Age, Survivor, and Disability Insurance.

11. This is from the 2005 report.

12. The Long Term Budget Outlook, 2005. The original CBO analysis assumed moving the retirement age to 67 for people born after 1949. However, with five years now gone by since the report was issued, that is five years of possible transition now lost. Because of these lost five years, we moved the retirement threshold to people born after 1954.

13. Geoffrey Kollmann, Domestic Social Policy Division, Congressional Research Service. "Social Security: Raising the Retirement Age Background and Issues." June 7, 2000.

14. "Social Security Formula Weighed." *Washington Post*, January 4, 2005.

15. Gregory Mankiw. "Social Security Reform: National Saving and Macroeconomic Performance in the Global Economy." Speech before the Council on Foreign Relations. January 18, 2005.

16. Jason Furman. Center on Budget and Policy Priorities. An analysis of using "progressive price indexing" to set Social Security benefits. May 2, 2005. This statistic is based on an analysis of progressive price indexing. A straight price indexing system would cut the gap even further.

17. Gregory Mankiw speech, January 18, 2005.

18. The matching rate varies from state to state. The wealthiest states receive a federal match of 50%, and poorer states receive an even larger match. In fact, Medicaid funding has become a huge budgetary issue for many states, with Medicaid expenditures consuming, on average, more than 20% of each state's budget.

chapter nine

Why ObamaCare Makes
Our Economy Sick

"What will [ObamaCare] mean for America? The short answer is that the reforms will expand coverage dramatically, but at a heavy cost to the taxpayer. They will also do far too little to rein in the underlying drivers of America's roaring health inflation. ... And that rate of spending was already unsustainable at a time when the baby-boomers are starting to retire in large numbers."

Economist (March 2010)[1]

President Barack Obama was right to pursue health care reform. America's costly health care system doesn't deliver enough value for the money spent. However, the legislation he slipped through Congress is just plain wrong.

Stripped of rhetoric, the Patient Protection and Affordable Care Act represents yet another inadequately funded entitlement program that will harm the American economy and the health care system. Indeed, by dramatically expanding health insurance coverage without adequately reining in America's out-of-control health care costs, ObamaCare has both weakened our health care system and put another brake on our long-term growth potential.

The fundamental question we must ask at this point is whether Congress should try to fix ObamaCare—or simply scrap it before it can do considerable damage.

Our strong recommendation is to start over. The key elements of ObamaCare—unreasonable mandates; heavy-handed insurance regulation; and entitlement-based, middle-income subsidies—must go. None of these elements addresses the fundamental problem of health care: high and rising costs.

Instead, the primary thrust of ObamaCare is simply to expand health-insurance coverage and pay for it in the worst two possible ways—by further increasing the budget deficit and by further raising taxes.

The Big Health Care Picture

In thinking about the big picture of health care, it is useful to reiterate the central message of this book: Long-term American economic prosperity cannot occur unless and until we address the massive structural imbalances in our GDP Growth Drivers equation. As we have seen, these structural imbalances have manifested themselves as a pattern of overconsumption, underinvestment, excess government spending, and chronic trade imbalances.

America's health care crisis contributes to these structural imbalances in at least three ways. First, we as Americans tend to "overconsume" health care services—typically, and ironically, without substantial added health care benefits. We do so because of a system of health insurance delivery practices and lucrative tax preferences that simultaneously subsidize employer-provided insurance and insulate us from the costs of health care consumption through low deductibles and low copayments.

Because of this system, right now $5 out of every $6 of health care spending is paid for by someone other than the person receiving care—the insurance company, the employer, or the government. We as individuals thereby are almost completely "price insensitive" in the health care services market and are largely separated from the reality of what our decisions cost. This lack of price sensitivity inevitably breeds overutilization of low-value health care and runaway spending.

The second way in which America's health care crisis exacerbates our economy's structural imbalances stems from the fact that health care costs are rising much faster than per capita GDP. As we saw in Chapter 8, "Cutting the Gordian Knot of Entitlements," these rising costs mean that Medicare and Medicaid expenditures are taking an ever-increasing share of our GDP. In this way, our health care crisis is further bloating our government sector.

The third way in which our health care crisis contributes to our structural imbalances stems from this sad fact of American political life: Because health care costs are rising so fast, politicians inevitably turn to raising taxes to finance programs such as Medicare and Medicaid. The latest politician to do so is, of course, President Obama. (This sin is bipartisan. Former President George W. Bush's Medicare expansion will require future tax increases unless we rein in Medicare spending.)

To help finance ObamaCare, the president has chosen the best possible tool to further *discourage* critically needed business investment. We refer, of course, to the significant tax hikes on upper-income earners, many of whom are small-business owners and entrepreneurs.

Under ObamaCare, the Medicare payroll tax will jump from 1.45% to 2.35% for upper-income filers.[2] At the same time, and even more injurious from a GDP growth drivers perspective, starting in 2013 ObamaCare will also slap a 3.8% tax on so-called "unearned income"—capital gains, interest income, and dividends. Note that this 3.8% tax on capital income is on top of another 5% tax hike that resulted from the Obama administration's allowing the 2001 and 2003 tax cuts to expire. *As a consequence, President Obama's tax hike on capital income will be 8.8 percentage points—an almost 60% jump.*

Of course, from a GDP growth drivers perspective, this tax hike will move us in exactly the opposite direction from long-term prosperity. It will depress rather than stimulate business investment—and thereby slow down the innovation, jobs, and increases in income that come from business investment.

For these three reasons, health care reform aimed at containing costs—and rebalancing our economy—is critical to America's long-term growth prospects. However, under ObamaCare, the only way to pay for these rising costs besides raising taxes will be to run ever-larger budget deficits or cut expenditures on other government programs such as defense or education. Of course, all these options are self-defeating if economic growth is our goal.

Are We Getting What We Are Paying For?

Evidence of the U.S. health care system's innovative strength is overwhelming. The Nobel Prize in Physiology or Medicine has been awarded to more Americans than to researchers in all other countries combined. Eight of the ten most important medical innovations of the past 30 years originated in the United States.[3] For cardiac and mental-health care, for example, few would like to turn back the medical-care clock to the 1950s, even if it meant they could spend the funds they saved on something else.

But the picture is not so positive for all health care spending. If spending an ever-larger share of our GDP on medical care were "worth it"—in the sense that such increased spending actually led to better health care—rising health spending would be much less of a concern. America's problem, however, is that a lot of its health care spending provides no measurable health benefits. In many cases, diagnostic procedures and tests are overutilized, procedures are employed without tangible results, and expensive pharmaceuticals are overprescribed.

Indeed, this is the paradox: Even though America spends almost twice as much per person on health care as many other major industrial countries, the quality of our health care—as measured by yardsticks as disparate as infant mortality, survival rates for major diseases, and deaths due to medical error—lags behind most other countries.

Exhibit 9.1 illustrates this paradox of high costs for sometimes relatively lower-quality care. It compares and contrasts key elements of the U.S. health care system with those of other major industrialized countries.

Exhibit 9.1   The Paradox of American Health Care: High(est) Costs Not Matched with Highest Value

Country	Life Expectancy	Infant Mortality Rate	Physicians Per 1,000 People	Per Capita Expenditures on Health (in U.S. Dollars)	Health Care Costs as a Percentage of GDP
Australia	81.4	4.2	2.8	3,137	8.7
Canada	80.7	5.0	2.2	3,895	10.1
France	81.0	4.0	3.4	3,601	11.0
Germany	79.8	3.8	3.5	3,588	10.4
Japan	82.6	2.6	2.1	2,581	8.1
Norway	80.0	3.0	3.8	5,910	9.0
Sweden	81.0	2.5	3.6	3,323	9.1
U.K.	79.1	4.8	2.5	2,992	8.4
U.S.	78.1	6.7	2.4	7,290	16.0

Source: Wikipedia, OECD.org. Life Expectancy versus Health Care Spending in 2007 for OECD Countries. http://www.oecd.org.

You can see that the United States leads all other countries by a wide margin in health expenditures as a percentage of GDP and per capita expenditures. However, you also can see that infant mortality rates in the United States are over two and a half times higher than in Sweden and Japan. We also rank last among the listed countries for life expectancy.

There is a clear market-driven path to reducing health care costs, while improving the quality of medical care. However, moving down this path will require individuals to take much greater responsibility for their health care. Health insurers and health care providers must also more fully face the competitive forces in the marketplace.

Toward this end, we propose three market-driven policy changes that would go a long way toward achieving the objectives of lower-cost and higher-quality care:

- Eliminating the tax code's bias that favors health insurance over out-of-pocket spending
- Removing state-government barriers to purchasing and providing health services
- A wide-ranging reform of medical malpractice laws

We estimate that these three changes alone would reduce health care costs by over $100 billion per year. However, before we examine these proposed changes, let's look at some of the major arguments for starting over on ObamaCare.

ObamaCare Puts the Coverage Cart Before the Cost Horse

"The Democrats have created another massive entitlement program while expanding federal power and reach in a manner not seen since the heyday of Franklin D. Roosevelt. If allowed to stand, the new health care law will tether America's middle class to the federal government in ways that will fundamentally alter—and not for the better—the relationship between citizens and the state. The result will be worse health care, distorted politics, less medical innovation and economic vitality, and depleted wealth."

Heritage Foundation (April 2010)[4]

The fundamental flaw of ObamaCare is that it puts the coverage cart before the cost containment horse. We believe that health insurance coverage for all Americans is important. However, adding another 30 million people to a health care system with poor incentives and without containing costs is like throwing more people into a lifeboat that is already sinking fast.

Exhibit 9.2, which is based on a study done by the RAND Corporation, illustrates how ObamaCare will actually *increase* health care costs beyond even the current, already high rate. These increased costs will arise from, among other factors, a combination of previously uninsured individuals using more health care services and, far more troublesome, previously insured people buying more generous plans in response to government subsidies.

Exhibit 9.2 ObamaCare Raises Health Care Costs

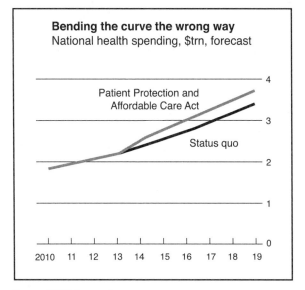

Source: RAND Corporation

ObamaCare Provides a Far-Too-Sweet Entitlement

In the same way that President Bush sweetened entitlement spending with his costly Medicare prescription drug bill, ObamaCare dramatically ups the entitlement ante by closing the so-called "donut hole" in the original Bush bill. Under the Bush drug plan giveaway, Medicare recipients pay 25% of the cost of prescription drugs up to $2,830 and only 5% of drug costs after $4,550. This upper threshold is called the "catastrophic cap." However, between $2,830 and $4,550, seniors have to pay 100% of the costs. This gap is the donut hole, and ObamaCare fills it by 2020.

Closing this donut hole is a sweeter-than Krispy-Kreme deal for seniors. They will pay only pennies on the dollar for their drugs. But two questions must be asked.

First, just who will pay for this lucrative new benefit? The president has no real answer, other than a cynical combination of "taxing the rich" and shifting the costs to our younger generations through higher payroll taxes and the accumulation of more and more government debt.

The second question is even more to the point: Why are we even offering such huge subsidies for *every* senior on Medicare, regardless of their levels of income and wealth? In fact, these huge blanket subsidies were precisely what was wrong with the Bush Medicare giveaway. Remember, Social Security and Medicare were originally supposed to be only *safety nets* for seniors, not indiscriminate entitlements.

Now, with features such as closing the donut hole and expanding coverage without the money to pay for it, ObamaCare will only make things worse—for our youth, our labor force, our middle-income households, and our economy.

Truth or Consequences

"Former Federal Reserve chief Alan Greenspan warns the economic impact of the new health care reform law could be disastrous if the Congressional Budget Office's (CBO) projections prove inaccurate. The real danger lies in the possibility the CBO underestimated the health care plan's actual real-world costs. Should the costs come in higher than projected, as many critics believe, the result would be increased borrowing by the federal government that could further damage the nation's credit and the economy in the long run."

Newsmax.com (April 2010)[5]

We are not sure which is worse about the 2010 health care law—the fact that the Obama administration employed a little-used parliamentary trick to ram through a piece of legislation that more than half the American public didn't support, or the fact that the Obama administration made false promises to shore up public support before the vote.

The first false promise was to claim that ObamaCare would actually reduce, rather than increase, our burgeoning federal budget deficits. To make this case, President Obama took out of context a study by the Congressional Budget Office.

In its report, the CBO claimed that ObamaCare would cost some $940 billion over the next decade. However, by generating additional tax revenues and cost savings, ObamaCare would also lead to a net *reduction* in the budget deficit of $138 billion. Could this be true? Actually, no. As former CBO director Douglas Holtz-Eakin wrote:

> "In reality, if you strip out all the gimmicks and budgetary games and rework the calculus, a wholly different picture

emerges: The health care reform legislation would raise, not lower, federal deficits, by $562 billion."[6]

Indeed, subsequent analyses by a wide range of analysts have revealed several fundamental flaws in the CBO study. This criticism is why former Federal Reserve Chairman Alan Greenspan has expressed such concern about the implications of the CBO's rosy scenario for long-term economic growth.

Arguably the most egregious false promise was this shell game: although ObamaCare starts taxing people almost immediately, the bulk of ObamaCare subsidies don't kick in until 2014. This "tax now, provide benefits later" feature dramatically skews the CBO's ten-year analysis. But that's not all. As Holtz-Eakin also noted:

> "Even worse, some costs are left out entirely. To operate the new programs over the first 10 years, future Congresses would need to vote for $114 billion in additional annual spending. But this so-called discretionary spending is excluded from the Congressional Budget Office's tabulation. ...Finally, in perhaps the most amazing bit of unrealistic accounting, the legislation proposes to trim $463 billion from Medicare spending and use it to finance insurance subsidies. But Medicare is already bleeding red ink, and the health care bill has no reforms that would enable the program to operate more cheaply in the future. Instead, Congress is likely to continue to regularly override scheduled cuts in payments to Medicare doctors and other providers."

In fact, once ObamaCare fully kicks in in 2014, the real cost of expanding coverage in the ten-year period from 2014 to 2023 will be more like $1.6 trillion, not $940 billion. Moreover, the result will be enlarged budget deficits in the hundreds of billions.

ObamaCare and the Law of Unintended Consequences

In addition to the big-picture problem of ObamaCare's increasing health care costs, a number of other problems stem from the well-known Law of Unintended Consequences.

One problem, which we refer to as the "51st employee problem," stems from the fact that small businesses are exempt from the government mandate to provide group health care so long as they employ 50 people or fewer. The obvious problem is the huge disincentive to hire that 51st employee, because the cost of doing so is far greater than the cost of the 51st employee's wages and benefits.

A second and related problem is that ObamaCare provides perverse incentives to businesses to cancel or diminish health care programs and push their employees into the government-run plans. This perverse incentive arises because it is actually much cheaper to simply pay the $2,000 per capita fine than it is to provide group insurance.

Still a third consequence of ObamaCare—unintended or not—is that it will shift the burden of paying for health care to our youth. As the Associated Press notes: "Under the health care overhaul, young adults who buy their own insurance will carry a heavier burden of the medical costs of older Americans—a shift expected to raise insurance premiums for young people when the plan takes full effect."[7] In fact, "premiums for young adults seeking coverage on the individual market would likely climb by 17% on average."[8] And, of course, today's youth will also pay tomorrow's ObamaCare taxes.

For all the reasons we have discussed, we strongly recommend starting over. We now turn to the task of how to begin reforming health care without harming our economy.

Toward a More Market-Driven Health Care System

> *"For every dollar's worth of health care that Americans received last year, they paid a dime and somebody else paid 90 cents. If you bought food the way you buy health care—where 90% of everything you put in your basket was paid for by your grocery insurance policy—you would eat differently and so would your dog. We have the best health care system in the world, but as rich as America is we can't afford it."*
>
> Former Senator Phil Gramm (March 2010)[9]

In our view, the unintended consequences of a handful of public policies are largely responsible for many of the problems of the health care system—particularly exploding costs. These policies share a common feature: They hinder, or otherwise fail to promote, the proper functioning of markets.

As noted earlier, three market-driven policy changes would go a long way toward achieving the objectives of lower-cost and higher-quality care:

- Eliminating the tax code's bias that favors health insurance over out-of-pocket spending
- Removing state-government barriers to purchasing and providing health services
- A wide-ranging reform of medical malpractice laws

The following sections discuss these policy changes in more detail.

Solution #1: Leveling the Tax Preference Playing Field

At the root of America's health care cost explosion is its employer-provided insurance system. Today, more than 175 million Americans in a population of about 300 million buy their health insurance through their workplace.[10]

The problem is not the employer-provided system *per se*. Rather, it is a set of highly lucrative tax subsidies or "tax preferences" that insulate consumers from the true costs and clear price signals of medical care. The resultant price-insensitivity of consumers leads to a whole range of wasteful medical practices and the overconsumption of low-value-added health care services.

This system of tax preferences for employer-paid health insurance costs began with a provision of the Stabilization Act of 1942 during World War II. As a wartime measure, this Act limited wage increases to contain inflation. However, the Act also permitted employer-paid health insurance to be provided as a fringe benefit exempt from wage controls. Whether or not it was intended, this provision allowed employers to compete for labor resources using "nonprice" tools such as offering tax-favored health care through group plans.

Shortly after its introduction, this tax preference was extended to the IRS tax code. In particular, under an administrative tax court ruling in 1954, employer contributions to employee health insurance costs officially became *deductible* for the employer and *nontaxable* for the employee.

Under today's system, neither employers nor employees pay income or payroll taxes on the employer's contribution to an employee's insurance plan. These tax preferences thereby create a strong financial incentive for individuals to purchase medical care through employer-provided insurance using *pretax* income. By contrast, a worker who purchases health insurance on his or her own must finance the purchase with *after-tax* income—income that remains after income and payroll taxes have been paid.

In fact, this system leads to a significant distortion in price signals. Consider that a typical middle-income worker faces a marginal federal income tax rate of about 15% and a payroll tax rate on wages of about 8%. An employer must also pay a payroll tax of about 8% on wages. Together, these various taxes raise the total marginal tax rate on wage income to approximately 30%. When an employee purchases health insurance through his or her employer, these taxes are avoided, and, together, employer and employee save almost one-third of the cost of the health care plan.

This tax subsidy is not the end of the story, however. The existence of these tax preferences creates large incentives for employees to purchase much more expensive employer-provided insurance plans with low deductibles and low copayments rather than "true insurance" plans geared primarily toward the coverage of catastrophic health events. The result is a high degree of price insensitivity to health care services.

Ultimately, then, the American health care system of tax preferences has institutionalized a classic problem of "moral hazard." Not only do consumers buy too much coverage, but the low deductibles and low coinsurance rates that characterize most employer-provided plans lead both patients and their physicians to use too many services that do little to improve measurable health outcomes.

The effects of such moral hazard on health care costs have been documented extensively, most notably by the RAND Corporation and the National Health Insurance Experiment.[11] For example, the RAND study found that people enrolled in catastrophic health plans *spend only about two-thirds as much* on medical care as those in full-coverage plans. Equally important, this study found that the health outcomes for those in the catastrophic plans were, with few exceptions, *no different than the outcomes for those on the full-coverage plan.*

A "Second-Best" Solution

Eliminating one of America's most enduring and lucrative tax preferences is, of course, a huge political hot potato. Eliminating the tax preference for employer-provided insurance would significantly raise taxes on any taxpayer who relies on employer-provided insurance—and, as noted, at last count this was over 170 million Americans.

To make this point clear, just consider a household facing a combined marginal and payroll tax rate of 30%. If this household contributes $6,600 to pay for its insurance plan, repealing the tax preferences would raise that household's taxes by $2,000.

Only former President Ronald Reagan expressed a willingness to consider repealing the health-insurance tax exclusion. In 1983, he proposed limiting the amount of employer-provided insurance that could be excluded from taxation, but his proposal was soundly rejected in Congress.

A similar proposal was considered and rejected during the 1985 tax reform debate. Since then, no president has proposed modifying the exclusion for employer-provided health insurance. Today, when Americans are registering unprecedented concerns about the high cost of health care, a policy that would significantly lower costs would likely face insurmountable legislative hurdles.

Given this high political hurdle, we propose a more palatable "second-best" way to address the clear bias toward employer-provided health plans. Simply put: Make all health spending tax-deductible—including out-of-pocket payments, purchases of individual insurance, and purchases of COBRA coverage.

Full deductibility would be especially helpful to individuals facing the high cost of chronic illness, and the unemployed who have lost their employer coverage. This could be accomplished with a single, sweeping policy change. It could also be achieved by expanding health savings accounts and flexible spending accounts, which also level the tax playing field between insured and out-of-pocket spending. That is, they make the tax treatment of insured and out-of-pocket spending more similar.

Allowing health care expenses to be tax-deductible will significantly reduce the growth in health costs as greater cost consciousness leads to less spending. Our proposal has other beneficial effects. Deductibility mitigates the tax bias against individual insurance, because both employer-sponsored and individual insurance can be acquired with preincome tax dollars. The tax change also enhances the fairness of the federal income tax system.[12] And allowing deductibility has very modest budget costs compared to ObamaCare.[13]

Solution #2: Loosening the Straitjackets of State Regulation

Our second set of reforms address several chronic and inherent problems in current state regulation of health care. At present, state health insurance regulations require insurers to cover certain types of care and restrict their ability to set premiums. These requirements and mandates raise insurance costs and limit the available range of insurance options. The result is perverse—higher numbers of uninsured people.

One state-level problem is with "mandated benefits laws." Such laws require health plans to cover particular types of people, services, or providers such as chiropractic services. Studies indicate that such mandates increase health insurance costs by at least 5%, and possibly as much as 15%, by muting market signals.

A second state-level problem is the existence of so-called "any willing provider" laws. These require health plans to accept bills from any doctor, hospital, or pharmacist who is willing to accept the plan's terms and conditions. Studies likewise increase costs by 1% to 2% by weakening the cost-containment effects of managed-care plans.

Still a third problem is that state-by-state regulation has raised costs by reducing competition among insurance companies. It has also allowed state legislatures to impose insurance mandates that raise prices while preventing residents from getting policies more suitable for their needs. The obvious solution is to allow individuals to buy health insurance offered in states other than those in which they live or in a national market.

Solution #3: Reforming the Malpractice System

"The United States loses more American lives to patient safety incidents every six months than it did in the entire Vietnam War. This also equates to three fully loaded jumbo jets crashing every other day for the last five years. Although not recognized as a cause of death by the Centers for Disease Control & Prevention (CDC) in its annual National Vital Statistics Report, if they were, medical errors would be ranked as the sixth leading cause of death in the United States and outrank deaths due to diabetes, influenza and pneumonia, Alzheimer's disease, and renal disease."

HealthGrades (July 2004)[14]

Research on medical malpractice litigation by both academics and government agencies is clear: Our excessive litigation system leads to fewer choices for patients and to higher costs because of "defensive medicine."

Defensive medicine refers to the practice of physicians ordering more diagnostic tests, procedures, and prescription drugs than might otherwise be dictated by a patient's profile. Physicians do so for fear of being sued, and this *directly* drives up costs.

Defensive medicine also *indirectly* raises costs by pushing up the cost of physician insurance. For example, doctors in states without reasonable limits on economic damages—including Nevada, Pennsylvania, Mississippi, North Carolina, Virginia, Florida, Ohio, and Illinois—have been subject to annual double-digit increases in malpractice premiums.

The irony of our malpractice litigation system is that it often leads to *more* rather than fewer medical errors. Given that medical errors are the leading cause of accidental death in the United States, this is no small irony.

Just what kinds of medical errors kill as many as 100,000 Americans a year? They range from misdiagnosing or failing to diagnose specific diseases to "wrong-site surgeries" such as amputating the wrong arm. Some of the worst medical errors include giving a patient the wrong drug or wrong dose or combining drugs in a way that causes poisonous byproducts to build up in the patient's system. Medical errors even involve leaving behind things such as sponges and gauze in a patient during surgery.

Just how does our malpractice system fuel this fire? The very existence of the malpractice system systematically suppresses the collection and analysis of precisely the kind of hospital and patient data that would otherwise help reduce medical errors. This situation is a peculiarly American tragedy.

Systems of error reporting, analysis, and feedback are essential to efforts to reduce medical errors. However, the biggest impediment to the creation and success of these systems is the possible discoverability of their data by potential plaintiffs in medical malpractice lawsuits. Because physicians legitimately fear that lawyers may use any information against them, they tend to collect much less of it and include much less of it in a patient's file.

A system-level failure also occurs: Although states provide varying levels of statutory protection for physicians, from the analysis of medical errors *within* individual health care organizations through peer-review protection laws, analyses that involve information sharing *across* organizations are largely unprotected.

By allowing plaintiffs to use quality-improvement initiatives against malpractice defendants, current law gives doctors, hospitals, and insurers a further disincentive to collect information on medical errors. But this is exactly the wrong signal to send. Public policy should encourage investment to reduce medical errors, not discourage it.

What Can Be Done?

As a first step to reforming the malpractice system, we propose a reasonable national cap on noneconomic damages in medical malpractice lawsuits. Reasonable caps would go a long way toward reducing costs and decreasing unnecessary defensive medicine.

Consistent with findings of the Institute of Medicine and many bills that have been introduced in Congress, we also propose to limit the discoverability of data on adverse events collected for purposes of quality improvement. Such legal protection will encourage health care organizations to develop policies to collect and analyze information about medical errors and will encourage doctors, nurses, and other health care workers to report mistakes. Passing such legislation would be an important step toward reducing medical errors.

We likewise believe that both patients and health care providers should be given more freedom to experiment with alternatives to litigation. One option that would lead to results that are faster and fairer and would lower transaction costs is alternative dispute resolution (ADR).

In the ADR process, patients and health care providers voluntarily submit disputes to an arbitrator, who resolves the case in a binding decision. Such an approach would replace the current compensation lottery with a more consistent decision-making process.

As a final reform of our malpractice system, we propose using a guidelines-based rule for adjudicating physician negligence and malpractice claims. Under the common law of most states, physician negligence is an issue of fact for the jury, informed by expert testimony.

In contrast, under a guidelines-based system, compliance with the guideline could be allowed as a defense to malpractice. Failure to comply with the guideline without a patient's written permission could be allowed as evidence of malpractice. Although guidelines are an obvious source of information about the negligence of a given treatment decision in a medical malpractice case, courts generally bar them from being admitted as evidence under the hearsay rule, which prohibits the introduction of out-of-court statements as evidence. However, because there are many contexts in which medical care is widely known to deviate from "best practices," expanding the role of guidelines has the potential to improve the quality of care further.

Conclusion

"Any real debate about health care reform has to be centered on solving the problem of cost. Ultimately, there are only two ways of doing it. The first approach is to have government control costs through some form of rationing. The alternative is to empower families to make their own health care decisions in a system where costs matter. The fundamental question is about who is going to do the controlling: the family or the government."

Former Senator Phil Gramm[15]

The three types of policies we propose offer considerable advantages over ObamaCare. Instead of raising health care costs, they fundamentally change incentives among individuals, insurers, and providers to gradually slow the growth in costs by reducing inefficient demand without sacrificing quality and innovation. Instead of radically changing health care overnight, they take an incremental approach, respecting the tremendous uncertainty surrounding the effectiveness of different approaches to rein in costs.[16]

As a final remark, we, like the Obama administration, believe that it is important to increase access to health care. However, this should not be confused with increasing access to health insurance. The most subtle but salient point is this: Increasing health care access—or growing our economy!—cannot be achieved responsibly without also getting health care costs under control.

That said, we believe several ideas for improving access are worth considering:

- Removing artificial barriers to entry for physicians and within specialty groups
- Allowing states greater flexibility with Medicaid (as we discussed in the last chapter)
- Providing tax credits for health spending
- Expanding programs that provide services directly, such as community health centers

In this regard, San Francisco has a promising alternative along these lines called Healthy San Francisco. It restructures the existing health care safety net system (both public and nonprofit) into a coordinated, integrated system.

Our bottom line is this: Despite the claims of some partisans to the contrary, ObamaCare does not speak to the concerns of the majority of Americans. Instead of addressing the high and rising costs of care, it establishes mandates, invasive regulation, and unaffordable new entitlements. This will not bring down health care costs; it will only make the problem worse.

In promising the "largest middle-class tax cut for health care in history," ObamaCare is simply a creative way of describing a vast tax-payer-subsidized insurance entitlement. The fine print leaves us with one of the largest tax increases for health care in history. The devil truly is in the details.

To close this chapter, we leave you with a quote from the state treasurer of Massachusetts, Timothy Cahill. Based on his experiences with a lighter variation of ObamaCare in his home state, Mr. Cahill had this to say:

> "While everyone should have access to affordable health care, our experience in Massachusetts tells us that the new federal entitlement will burden future taxpayers with unfunded liabilities they cannot afford. Health care inflation will continue. Mandates will increase insurance premiums. And the deficit will reach frightening levels as the law's costs greatly exceed the projections of its advocates."[17]

Endnotes

1. "Signed, sealed, delivered." *The Economist*. March 25, 2010.

2. For individuals the threshold is $200,000, and for couples it is $250,000.

3. Victor R. Fuchs and Harold Sox, "Physicians' Views of the Relative Importance of Thirty Medical Innovations, "*Health Affairs* 20 (2001): 30-42.

4. "The Long War of Repealing ObamaCare." *The Heritage Foundation*. April 6, 2010.

5. Newsmax.com. "Greenspan: If CBO Numbers Wrong, ObamaCare Disastrous." April 5, 2010.

6. Douglas Holtz-Eakin. "The Real Arithmetic of Health Care Reform." *New York Times*. March 20, 2010.

7. Carla K. Johnson (AP). "Health premiums could rise 17 pct for young adults." March 29, 2010.

8. Ibid.

9. Phil Gramm. "Resistance Is Not Futile." *Wall Street Journal*. March 25, 2010.

10. Income, Poverty, and Health Insurance Coverage in the United States: 2007. U.S. Census Bureau. August 2008.

11. J. P. Newhouse and the Insurance Experiment Group. *Free for All? Lessons from the RAND Health Insurance Experiment*. Cambridge, Massachusetts: Harvard University Press, 1993.

12. Although marginal tax rates are higher for higher-income people, the fact that lower-income people have higher (currently taxable) out-of-pocket spending more than compensates for this effect.

13. Tax deductibility would create a revenue loss by making currently taxed health spending deductible. However, tax deductibility would also lead to a shift in how medical care is purchased, away from insurance and toward out-of-pocket expenses, and a reduction in overall spending. Lower insurance costs to employers would shift compensation to wages: Just as increases in health insurance costs are borne by workers in the form of lower wages, decreases would accrue to them as higher wages, which would be subject to both income and payroll taxes, raising revenue. The net cost is modest; see John F. Cogan, R. Glenn Hubbard, and Daniel P. Kessler, *Healthy, Wealthy, and Wise: Five Steps to a Better Health Care System* (Washington, DC, AEI Press, 2005).

14. "Patient Safety in American Hospitals." Study released by *HealthGrades*. July 2004.

15. Gramm, 2010.

16. For an even more detailed discussion of the various policies described in this chapter, see John F. Cogan, R. Glenn Hubbard, and Daniel P. Kessler. *Healthy, Wealthy, and Wise: Five Steps to a Better Health Care System*. The AEI Press, American Enterprise Institute, Washington, DC, 2005.

17. Timothy Cahill. "Massachusetts Is Our Future." *Wall Street Journal*. March 25, 2010.

PART V

The American Economy at a Crossroads

In analyzing financial reform in Chapter 10, "How to Prevent Another Financial Crisis—and Housing Bubble," we explain just how the bursting of a housing bubble managed to trigger the worst recession since the Great Depression and bring the entire global financial system to the brink of collapse. We then turn to a sobering critique of the sweeping "reforms" passed by the American Congress in response—and explain why much of this massive piece of legislation misses the mark. Following an Occam's Razor approach, we illustrate how a far simpler, and far less intrusive, set of reforms would do a far better job of preventing any future financial crises.

Chapter 11, "How to Implement Our Seeds of Prosperity Policy Blueprint," concludes the book with a summary of, and final thoughts about, our Seeds of Prosperity policy blueprint.

chapter ten

How to Prevent Another Financial Crisis—and Housing Bubble

"It is essential that we learn the lessons of the crisis, so we don't doom ourselves to repeat it."

President Barack Obama (April 2010)[1]

AIG, CDO, MBS—OMG! Just how did the bursting of a mere housing bubble trigger the worst recession since the Great Depression and bring the entire global financial system to the brink of collapse?

That's a good question. And President Obama's observation is right—addressing a serious crisis requires stepping back. Unfortunately, the president didn't move beyond the bully pulpit of asking questions to leading a search for solutions.

Only by coming up with some precise answers can we design a regulatory reform package that will truly insulate us from the repeat of any such shock. However, we must be careful here—particularly in the face of widespread public anger and equally widespread support for tougher regulations to punish a "greedy" Wall Street and a "profligate" corporate America. As we noted in Chapter 3, "Why an Easy-Money Street Is a Dead End," there were many underlying causes of the financial crisis, including low real interest rates in international capital markets that encouraged risk-taking.

But government policies also played a role: We must be careful because it was not "too little regulation" that caused the financial crisis. Witness the role of regulation's heavy hand in the fall of government-sponsored entities such as Fannie Mae and Freddie Mac or in encouraging banks to lend to subprime borrowers. Rather, it was the lack of *effective* regulation in the face of a set of overwhelmingly powerful perverse incentives that led so many actors in the housing bubble drama to go astray.

Thinking about what we mean by effective regulation requires us to set goals. Financial regulation should reduce the likelihood of crises but preserve healthy innovation. The failure to understand these points has resulted in yet another massive piece of legislation by the Obama administration that widely misses the mark. This legislation, the Wall Street Reform and Consumer Protection Act—popularly known as the "Dodd-Frank Act" for its primary authors, Sen. Christopher Dodd (D-CT) and Representative Barney Frank (D-MA)—represents an equally massive expansion of the government bureaucracy. It establishes no fewer than five new government agencies and entities. The legislation also fails to reduce the chance that "too big to fail" dinosaurs again will wreak financial havoc and drain the public purse.

We strongly prefer an Occam's Razor approach in which "entities must not be multiplied beyond necessity." Following this metatheoretical principle, the 14th century English logician William of Ockham concluded that the simplest solution is usually the correct one. Of course, nothing is simple about the new financial reform law. We believe, however, that there is a much more simple and direct route to preventing any reoccurrence of a 2007–2009 financial crisis. To find that route—and the real reforms that should be adopted—it is useful to systematically work our way through the 11 major causes of the crisis.

#1: Easy Money

The U.S. housing bubble and its recessionary aftermath were importantly influenced by the ultra-easy money policies of the U.S. Federal Reserve. As we discussed at length in Chapter 3, the U.S. Federal Reserve laid part of the groundwork for the creation of the housing bubble by maintaining artificially low interest rates for an extended period in the wake of the tragedy of 9/11. After the Federal Reserve should have been raising interest rates according to metrics such as the Taylor Rule, Fed Chairman Alan Greenspan kept interest rates artificially low for an extended period. Fed Chairman Ben Bernanke is continuing this "tonic" even as the U.S. economy recovers from the financial crisis.

It follows that in thinking about any massive restructuring of our regulatory apparatus to prevent a future housing crisis—and to begin to understand why the new financial reform law was such an overreach—we need to first take a deep breath. The fact is this most recent crisis—and any massive regulatory overhaul—would have been partially averted by following a less accommodative monetary policy.

This conclusion is not quite the end of the Federal Reserve story, however. The failure of both the Bush and Obama administrations to move swiftly and boldly during the financial crisis forced the Bernanke Fed to expand its lending and balance sheet, stretching the limits of prudence. This action more than doubled the size of that balance sheet and has yet to reduce it.

This bloated balance sheet has raised concerns about both the Fed's independence and future inflation. That's why we believe that any existing Fed loans to the private sector that are insufficiently collateralized (such as those in the Bear Stearns and AIG bailouts) should be removed from the Fed's balance sheet. Then they should be transferred to the federal balance sheet, where they belong. The new law failed to force this transfer, an important policy omission.

#2: Not Enough "Skin in the Game" for American Home Buyers

"To obtain a conventional mortgage, home buyers are required to put down at least 20% of the purchase price or appraised value (whichever is less) as a down payment. If you don't have the necessary time or resources to save a full 20% down payment, you can choose a high-ratio mortgage and buy a home with as little as a 5% down payment. This option is called a high-ratio mortgage and it requires you to purchase default insurance."

TD Canada Trust Bank[2]

Low money down. Even no money down. Come on down!

These were the "no skin in the game" rules of the home-buying game—at least in America—as the housing bubble began to form in the mid-2000s. Because many new home buyers had little or no equity in their homes when the housing bubble burst and home prices collapsed, it was as easy as putting one foot in front of the other for these people to just walk away and leave the keys in the mailbox. As a result, they also left whoever was holding their mortgage (and mortgage-backed securities and collateralized debt obligations!) holding the bag.

Even when home buyers initially had significant equity in their homes, loose lending practices allowed them to remove this equity through mortgage refinancing. America's "refi boom" during the height of the housing bubble effectively turned the American home into not just a casino but also an ATM. Too many Americans took too much equity out of their homes. Then, when the housing bubble burst and home prices collapsed, they too had little or no incentive to continue paying their mortgage on a home that was, at least figuratively, "underwater."

The stark Occam's Razor fact here is that the housing bubble in America would have inflated much less if homeowners had been required to put down at least 20% on any home purchase—or to purchase mortgage loan insurance. This approach is precisely the one taken in Canada. It is certainly no coincidence that even during the height of the housing bubble collapse, the rate of foreclosures in Canada was far lower than in the United States. Unfortunately, its more than 1,300 pages notwithstanding, the new law failed to address this critical reform.

Of course, any such regulatory requirement will have its critics. They will argue that the requirement will penalize first-time and low-income home buyers. That may be true, but if this is the policy concern—and it is a legitimate concern—there are far better ways to assist these home buyers (say, through direct subsidies) and target markets than having a regulatory regime in which home buyers can enter the market with "no skin in the game" and therefore have little incentive to stay in the game when things go south.

#3: Not Enough "Skin in the Game" for Mortgage Lenders

"Before Washington Mutual collapsed in the largest bank failure in U.S. history, its executives knowingly created a 'mortgage time bomb' by making subprime loans they knew were likely to go bad and then repackaging them into risky securities, a congressional investigation has found.

Consider these two situations. First, a bank or financial institution provides a mortgage to a home buyer and keeps all, or a significant portion, of that mortgage in its portfolio. Second, in a situation known as the "originate to distribute" model, a bank or financial institution provides a mortgage to a home buyer. However, the institution immediately sells that mortgage into the broader mortgage market and does not service it.

In which situation do you think the bank or financial institution will be more careful about making that loan? The answer is obvious. When a bank or financial institution plans to hang on to a mortgage, it has a vested interest in making sure that the house in question has been appraised properly, that the borrower has enough income to meet his or her monthly payments, and that all parties to the transaction have faithfully and truthfully provided answers to all questions pertaining to the loan.

In fact, at the height of the housing bubble, bad actors descended on the housing market like a plague of locusts in large part because lenders had no real "skin in the game." Just as home buyers were flipping houses, mortgage lenders were issuing, and then flipping, mortgages.

In large part because of the permissive atmosphere created by mortgage lenders, all manner of stakeholders acted with little or no regard for either the letter of the law or any meaningful sense of corporate ethics. Some real estate brokers lied about the value of homes. Some real estate appraisers, working in league with the eager brokers, routinely inflated the value of homes to facilitate issuing mortgages. Some mortgage lenders routinely failed to engage in any due diligence with respect to checking reported income levels, job status, and borrower assets. And, of course, some prospective home buyers lied about their balance sheets and provided forged or fraudulent documents ranging from tax returns to the verification of rental payments.

It follows from these observations that, like homeowners, mortgage originators and securitizers should be required to have some "skin in the game." That is, mortgage originators and securitizers should be required to retain at least some of the credit risks of the structures they create. At least, the new financial regulation law understood this. It included a "risk retention requirement" provision, and allows the amount of risk retained to depend on the quality of underwriting.

#4: Way-Too-Exotic Mortgages for Borrowers

"An Adjustable Rate Mortgage, or ARM, easily can force a bankruptcy filing. We call it an 'exploding' ARM, because the adjustment blows up the interest rate into the stratosphere, as most recent ARMs will do."

Bankruptcy Law Network (November 2007)[4]

The housing bubble era marked an important period in American financial history during which the practice of "creative finance" turned into "destructive finance." Nowhere was this transformation more evident than in the proliferation of the wide range of exotic subprime mortgage lending instruments that effectively allowed some people who could not afford to buy a house to do just that. Subprime lending is not a bad thing in and of itself, but its execution drew in far too many unqualified borrowers. Moreover, even some home buyers who might otherwise have had no difficulty qualifying for a traditional, fixed-rate home loan with a significant down payment were seduced into loans. Down the road these could, at least figuratively, explode in their faces.

The most common of these instruments was the adjustable-rate mortgage. Prior to the housing bubble, the overwhelming majority of Americans relied on fixed-rate mortgages—and the certainty of the monthly payments they could count on. However, as the housing bubble grew, adjustable-rate mortgages, often with very low "teaser rates," became more the rule rather than the exception.

Worst among these adjustable-rate mortgages was the so-called "exploding ARM." With this type of mortgage, monthly payments are often set at a very low *initial interest rate*—the so-called "teaser"—and well below a combination of the eventual *base rate* and a *margin*. Somewhere between one month and several years after the mortgage begins, the rate jumps, often significantly. At this point, this "explosion" in a home buyer's monthly payments can often lead to insolvency.

Just why did some home buyers get sucked into exploding ARMs? Often, it was simply because they could not afford the monthly payments on a 30-year fixed-rate mortgage. So they gambled that home prices would continue to escalate and that they would eventually be able to refinance their home and take advantage of the increase in equity. Of course, when home prices plunged, this was not quite the exit strategy they planned for.

Another type of exotic instrument is the "balloon mortgage." This mortgage must be paid in full within a set time, typically five years. Such a mortgage is actually made for house flippers and speculators. They buy a house fully expecting to sell it within the time period—or much sooner. However, once housing prices began to fall, many balloon mortgage holders were left holding the bag. Foreclosure was just a matter of time.

Still a third type of exotic instrument is the "interest-only loan." Here, the homeowner pays only interest and does not build up any equity during the initial period. Often used in conjunction with adjustable-rate mortgages, interest-only loans provide rock-bottom interest rates at the outset of the mortgage. They thereby facilitate the entry of home buyers who otherwise would be unable to afford the mortgage. Of course, with this kind of structure, it was only a matter of time before economic realities would catch up with the mortgage borrower. This observation was particularly true as soon as housing prices started to decline, and it made getting rid of the house through a sale sufficient to cover the mortgage difficult or impossible.

A final type of exotica of note were so-called "liar loans." For such a mortgage, no documentation was required. Such loans were justified in the case of self-employed people, because documenting their pay history might be difficult. Although these loans typically carried higher interest rates, these higher rates did not in any way upset the risk of default, because in many cases, the liar loans provided a back door for people with abysmal credit.

Prior to 2001, these various types of exotic loans were virtually unknown and comprised less than 5% of the overall loan volume. However, between 2001 and 2006, high-risk subprime lending rose from 5.8% of total mortgage originations to 23.5%. So-called "Alt-A mortgages," which are only slightly less risky than subprime mortgages, rose from 2.9% to 15.7%.

It is debatable just how many home buyers actually understood the full and significant risks involved in participating in such destructive finance. Some say that most home buyers were duped by the mortgage lenders and therefore are not really to blame for what happened. Others say that most home buyers fully understood the risks they were taking, and they should bear the responsibility of any debts gone bad.

We think that the truth is likely somewhere in the middle. On the one hand, many gamblers and home flippers during the height of the housing bubble relied on exotic lending instruments to effectively leverage their household balance sheet. On the other hand, we are not so naive as to believe that the American public as a group is particularly well educated about the intricacies of economics and finance. The question, of course, is just how much consumers need to be "protected" from unscrupulous real estate brokers, appraisers, and mortgage lenders.

We believe the best answer to this question lies not in the creation of a huge Consumer Protection bureaucracy, as the new law has done. Rather, we believe the answer lies in the far simpler and more direct prohibition or restriction of high-risk mortgage products and lending practices, particularly insofar as access to the securitization markets is concerned. And regulators must go beyond merely pushing for better risk management practices. They must prescribe substantive rules governing residential mortgage products and underwriting.

#5: The Mortgage-Backed Securities Meltdown

"On Wall Street, they were all known as 'quants,' traders and financial engineers who used brain-twisting math and superpowered computers to pluck billions in fleeting dollars out of the market. Instead of looking at individual companies and their performance, management and competitors, they use math formulas to make bets on which stocks were going up or down. By the early 2000s, such tech-savvy investors had come to dominate Wall Street, helped by theoretical breakthroughs in the application of mathematics to financial markets, advances that had earned their discoverers several shelves of Nobel Prizes."

Scott Patterson, *Wall Street Journal* (January 2010)[5]

The 2007–2009 financial crisis was not the first time expert financial engineers almost brought the global financial system to its knees with some innovative financial instruments that performed a lot better in theory than in practice. The first time this happened was during the 1997–1998 Asian financial meltdown.

During this crisis, two business school professors who shared the 1997 Nobel Prize in Economics—Myron Scholes and Robert C. Merton—were the grand strategists for a hedge fund known as Long-Term Capital Management. This hedge fund used complex mathematical models developed by Scholes and Merton to essentially run an arbitrage game typically involving European, Japanese, and American bonds. At one point, LTCM was generating annual returns in excess of 40%.

However, when Russia unexpectedly defaulted on its own government bonds, there was a panic sell-off of both Japanese and European bonds, and investors flocked to the safety of U.S. Treasury bonds. The heavily leveraged Long-Term Capital Management experienced initial losses from this panic sell-off that were close to $2 billion, because its managers had failed to fully price in the risk of its strategy.

As the hedge fund's losses continued to mount and it was forced to further liquidate additional positions, the U.S. Federal Reserve feared a chain reaction in global financial markets whereby further losses would force other companies to also begin liquidating their positions. At this point, the U.S. Federal Reserve stepped in and organized a bailout involving a number of major banks such as J.P. Morgan and Goldman Sachs.

This story is worth telling in some detail precisely because few on Wall Street or in Washington seemed to learn much of anything from it. The obvious moral of this story is that complex mathematical models are fallible and liquidity cannot be taken for granted—but this lesson was not brought into the 21st century.

In the 2007–2009 crisis, flawed mathematical models working in conjunction with a host of new and equally exotic financial instruments likewise helped contribute mightily to the crisis. One such instrument was known as the mortgage-backed security (MBS).

In its simplest form, an MBS is a bond backed by a pool of mortgages that are paid by homeowners. Bondholders essentially buy the cash flow from all the mortgage payments made by homeowners in the pool. Thus, every time a homeowner makes a payment, it is sent to the bondholder. In this way, the MBS holder effectively receives an interest payment plus a partial repayment of the principal. MBSs offer benefits of pooling and risk sharing, and can lower costs of housing finance.

But, as a practical matter, during the housing bubble most mortgage-backed securities were issued either by government-sponsored entities such as Fannie Mae and Freddie Mac or by financial institutions such as Countrywide, Lehman Brothers, Citigroup, and J.P. Morgan. Of course, when more and more homeowners began to default on mortgages, Fannie Mae and Freddie Mac—which had guaranteed the securities—had to step in and provide the missing cash flow. Thus, it should be no surprise that both Fannie Mae and Freddie Mac required such a massive bailout to stay solvent.

One clear lesson from the bailouts of Fannie Mae and Freddie Mac is that it is inappropriate for these government-sponsored entities to allow their shareholders to benefit from high risk-taking while taxpayers are forced to bail them out anytime such risk-taking goes bad. One possibility is to guarantee their securities explicitly—in place of the present implicit guarantee—but prohibit the firms from taking the balance-sheet risk that brought them to the brink of collapse.

The Obama administration offers no guidance in this situation. If we are to have a public presence here, it should be transparent, and Fannie and Freddie should hedge their balance sheet risk.

#6: The Collateralized Debt Obligations Credit Rating Debacle

"Goldman Sachs Group Inc. was sued by U.S. regulators for fraud tied to collateralized debt obligations that contributed to the worst financial crisis since the Great Depression. ...Goldman Sachs created and sold CDOs linked to subprime mortgages in early 2007, as the U.S. housing market faltered, without disclosing that hedge fund Paulson & Co. helped pick the underlying securities and bet against the vehicles, the Securities and Exchange Commission said today."

Bloomberg News (April 2010)[6]

A hefty portfolio of failing mortgage-backed securities was a root cause of the Fannie Mae and Freddie Mac bailouts. But a second type of exotic instrument—the collateralized debt obligation (CDO)—helps explain the collapse of Wall Street icons such as Bear Stearns and Lehman Brothers.

You can think of a CDO as a mortgage-backed security on steroids. Most of them were issued by major financial institutions such as Citigroup, Merrill Lynch, and UBS.

Technically, a CDO consists of a pool of assets such as mortgages that are held by some corporate entity. This entity then "slices and dices" the asset pool by characteristics such as risk. The result is a set of what are called "tranches," which are organized by the order in which they are repaid with the cash flow from the assets. Thus, the first tranche is the least risky, because it has first access to the cash flow and thereby pays the lowest return. The last tranche is the most risky and earns the highest yield.

But a problem arose with many of the CDOs that were created. Just as with the Long-Term Capital Management debacle, the mathematical models used to price the CDOs systematically underestimated the considerable risk embedded in their structure. The underlying problem was that even the most senior tranches—the ones that were supposed to be the least risky—were based on sub-prime loans whose default probabilities were hard to ascertain.

CDO investors were told by highly reputable credit agencies such as Dun & Bradstreet, Fitch, Moody's Investor Service, and Standard & Poor's that their CDO securities were low-risk, "investment grade." Of course, when the housing bubble burst and home prices began their long and steady decline, the value of many CDOs imploded. Because many financial institutions had invested in CDOs using heavy leverage, they were stuck holding a big bag of debt.

An important example of this problem was one of Wall Street's first major casualties—and bailouts of the financial crisis—Bear Stearns. The company had a huge portfolio of CDOs that it had acquired with an astonishing amount of leverage that exceeded 30 to 1. Once its CDO bets began to go south, likelihood of survival was doomed.

It follows from these observations that one obvious set of reforms must focus on ensuring more accurate credit ratings. Indeed, because credit-rating agencies (CRAs) serve as gatekeepers for the global credit markets, they occupy a unique place in our financial system. The ratings provided by CRAs on structured finance securities facilitated the issuance of over $6.5 trillion into the global credit markets in the boom between 2005 and 2007.

One reason why the CRAs failed to deliver accurate assessments of the true risks of collateralized debt obligations is that they used a set of mathematical models that worked in theory but failed in the real world. And the failure of the major CRAs to assess accurately the risk associated with fixed-income securities tied to U.S. residential mortgages—a failure they shared, of course, with many financial institutions—played a significant role in the catastrophic losses for investors who relied on their ratings.

We believe that regulation should require far greater disclosure of what information credit ratings are based on—particularly for structured finance securities—to enhance the ability of investors and other market participants to assess and monitor ratings accuracy. To this end, we propose that CRAs should be required to completely disclose the criteria, methodologies, models, processes, key assumptions, and scenario analyses that they employ in rating all types of securities. Allowing for diverse views on credit risk from a broad range of investors will enable a more effective check on ratings accuracy than relying solely on unsolicited ratings from other CRAs.

The new law does improve the governance of the credit ratings industry. Establishing Sarbanes-Oxley-type governance controls for rating agencies is a good idea because they (like auditors) perform a key "gatekeeper" role for financial markets. And a separate stricter oversight makes sense. Despite these positive features, the new law encourages litigation—a boon for the plaintiffs' bar and a cost to investors—instead of urging the SEC to do its job.

#7: A Flawed Insurance Market: Credit Default Swaps

"Just as flood insurance encourages people to build houses on floodplains, bond default protection increased the willingness of investors to buy complex mortgage-backed securities even if they did not fully understand the risks involved."

Robert Pozen, *Too Big To Save* (2010)[7]

Collateralized debt obligations played a key role in the collapse of the housing bubble and the ensuing financial crisis. However, they would not have done nearly as much damage without the existence of another exotic lending instrument—the credit default swap (CDS).

What is so interesting is that even though the credit rating agencies were rating many collateralized debt obligations as investment grade, at least some investors didn't believe these ratings and decided to take out insurance in case the CDO defaulted. This insurance took the form of a credit default swap.

In theory, the credit default swap is a useful financial instrument. It allows investors to hedge the risk that a bond will default.[8] However, one problem that CDSs caused for the financial crisis is that the issuers of the swaps underestimated the risk of default—again because the underlying mathematical models used to price the bonds didn't accurately assess risk.

In fact, the far largest issuer of credit default swaps was the insurance giant AIG. It issued billions of swaps under the flawed assumption that it was taking on virtually no risk. But in fact it was concentrating massive financial risk inside the firm. The result, of course, was that AIG effectively became a ward of the state in the largest bailout in U.S. history once collateralized debt obligations began going into default and AIG had to begin paying its insurance.

From this story, one might conclude that the best path to reform is to ban CDSs. However, this is not our message at all. In fact, CDSs are important tools for both measuring and diversifying credit risk.

In fact, we believe that the principal problem is that the current structure of the CDS market leaves that market with significant potential to contribute to broader systemic risk through a "chain reaction" of defaults. In this regard, understanding the nature and dangers of systemic risk is critical to understanding the need for regulatory reform. Allow us this brief digression:

Systemic risk is the risk of collapse of an entire system or entire market, exacerbated by links and interdependencies, in which the failure of a single entity or cluster of entities can cause a cascading failure. In fact, the most compelling justification for financial regulation is the need to reduce systemic risk.

It was in the name of systemic risk that the federal government stepped in and bailed out big institutions ranging from AIG and Bear Stearns to Fannie Mae and Freddie Mac. The exception to the rule of the bailout—the failure to save Lehman Brothers and the chaos that followed in world financial markets—also helps underscore the dangers of systemic risk.

We believe that the federal government acted in far too much haste and was far too generous in its bailouts of many of the institutions it saved. However, we are also keenly aware of the dangers of systemic risk. Accordingly, as we move back to our discussion of appropriate reforms, we believe that a "centralized clearinghouse" for credit derivatives is a crucial step toward reducing systemic risk on a global scale.

Such a clearinghouse wouldn't just limit counterparty risk and eliminate obvious process and settlement problems. It also would enhance the liquidity and transparency of the CDS market by actively managing daily collateral requirements of clearinghouse members and the netting of positions between and among them.

Unfortunately, although the Treasury Department has pledged to subject all standardized over-the-counter (OTC) derivative contracts—particularly CDSs—to centralized clearing, it has, at least thus far, exercised little leadership in making this happen.

The new law makes progress here.

Nonetheless, the new financial reform law punts on key derivatives issues, giving excessive discretion to regulators. Although central clearing and exchange trading should be required for standardized and liquid contracts, the law gives the Commodity Futures Trading Commission and Securities and Exchange Commission complete discretion to require that any and all derivative contracts be accepted for clearing. This sweeping discretion could eliminate, or make much more costly, key hedging activities. With its focus on systemic risk, the Federal Reserve is in the best position to have regulatory authority over derivatives regulation. The new law again punts on making a jurisdictional call.

#8: Inflexible Bank Capital

Historically, regulating the level of a financial institution's capital reserves has been the dominant means to constrain bank risk-taking—and it's easy to see why. By providing a cushion against losses, capital reserves are supposed to act as a first line of defense against bank failures and their knock-on consequences for systemic risk. Yet, the existing capital regime—particularly rules about holding capital reserves—failed to prevent several of the largest financial institutions from failing or becoming distressed to the point where they needed to be bailed out by the government.

Until the crisis, firms that were not regulated as banks (or thrifts) and that were not subject to capital regulation were excluded from the Fed's safety net. The Fed's emergency measures during the crisis have upended this understanding. These measures may have been justified by the far-out circumstances of the crisis, but they have created moral hazard and impediments to a level playing field, to the extent that institutions with access to the Fed safety net are not subject to capital regulation. Looking beyond the crisis, we need to realign the institutional costs and benefits of capital regulation.

We believe that institutions that can borrow from the Fed in its role as lender of last resort should be subject to some form of capital regulation.

One of the most important flaws of the current regulatory framework for setting minimum capital levels is that reserve levels are fixed rather than flexible over the course of the business cycle. This inflexibility forces banks to raise capital in a business cycle downturn, and as losses mount, capital levels are depleted. The result is that any contraction in the economy is further amplified by an increasing inability of the banks to lend.

We propose a key revision to the existing capital framework. This change would involve a shift to business cycle-sensitive capital requirements to avoid a boom-bust cycle from inflexible capital limits. There are several ways to implement such a reform.

One alternative is to require financial institutions to build up reserves during booms. A second alternative is to raise contingent capital during a downturn by converting unsecured debt to equity.

Thus far, the crisis has disproportionately affected the largest U.S. financial institutions. At the same time, the initial capital injections from the Troubled Assets Relief Program were also concentrated in the largest U.S. banks. Large institutions pose unique risks to the government because of their systemic consequences. As a result—and this is our bottom line—large or important banks (from a systemic failure point of view) should be required to hold a larger capital buffer.

#9: Too Big to Fail: Last Rites for Financial Dinosaurs

"Amid last fall's financial chaos, executives from Wachovia, at the time the fourth-largest commercial bank in the country, had bad news for their regulators: They were broke. Federal officials deliberated and decided Wachovia was so important to the economy that the government had to save it.

"It was only the latest in a series of financial institutions that regulators had deemed 'too big to fail.' In the preceding months, the government had bailed out Fannie Mae, Freddie Mac, and Bear Stearns, and Congress had passed the controversial $700 billion bill to fund yet more financial-sector rescues. Some of the institutions, like the insurance company American International Group (AIG), weren't even banks."

American Prospect (October 2009)[9]

As the failure of Lehman and the rescue of AIG indicated, we have had significant trouble resolving the failure of big, complicated financial institutions. This brick in the wall of "too big to fail" must be replaced. Otherwise, we will repeat the destructive process of massive bailouts that we witnessed during the last crisis.

Current law for banks creates a flexible insolvency regime that provides for pre-resolution action and many methods of resolution, including liquidation, open bank assistance, purchase and assumption transactions, and the establishment of bridge banks. This regime has been successful in promoting stability in the banking system. It has reduced uncertainty for depositors and counterparties while successfully mitigating losses for banks, counterparties, and the deposit insurance fund. However, this regime is available only to resolve *banks*. It excludes from coverage many systemically significant financial companies, including bank holding companies.

Recently, the Obama Treasury proposed the creation of an additional insolvency regime with powers similar to those available for banks that can be invoked when a financial company's insolvency poses a systemic risk to market. The Treasury's proposals are inadequate. A better alternative is the implementation of a comprehensive Financial Company Resolution Act, based on banking rules, that is applicable to all financial institutions.

The new financial reform law, while too big to read, offers little to deal with the elephant in the room of too-big-to-fail. While the law tackles resolution authority, it lacks key specifics. At least the law jettisoned the Obama administration's call to capitalize a large "orderly liquidation fund" in advance, an open invitation to bailouts. That's why this should be done on an as-needed basis, with creditors and counterparties of failed institutions bearing resolution costs over a medium term.

#10: A Fragmented and Sectoral Model of Regulation

Most other leading financial center countries have moved toward consolidated financial oversight. But the United States remains saddled with a fragmented and sectoral model of regulation. This model was woefully unprepared to deal with the 2007–2009 financial crisis and all the problems of widespread systemic risk it entails. The clear lesson from the crisis—and the exceedingly slow reaction times of our key but fragmented regulatory institutions—is that effective financial regulation going forward will inevitably require a reorganization of the current regulatory structure.

In reviewing the wreckage of the crisis, the January 2009 Report of the Committee on Capital Markets Regulation (cochaired by one of us) recommended important changes in regulatory responsibilities. These are appropriate for the regulatory bodies in a system of consolidated oversight. In the new structure, the Fed would retain its exclusive control of monetary policy and its lender-of-last-resort function as part of its key role in ensuring financial stability.

Note that this recommendation is in sharp contrast to current proposals to vest systemic risk regulation in an interagency council composed of several existing regulatory agencies. We believe this is dead wrong and that this important role should be retained by the Fed. We believe this for the simple but powerful reason that one regulator, and one regulator alone, needs both the authority and accountability to regulate matters pertaining to systemic risk.

In addition, we propose a new U.S. Financial Services Authority (USFSA) that would regulate all aspects of the financial system, including market structure and activities and safety and soundness for all financial institutions (and possibly consumer and investor protection with respect to financial products if this responsibility were lodged with the USFSA).

Assuming that the better option of a fully consolidated regulator is off the table—as the new financial reform law envisions—the law's Consumer Finance Protection Agency should be independent. The placement of the agency in the Fed is cynical—to obtain Fed funding from the profits the Fed makes from monetary policy and other services (over $50 billion in 2009). These funds would normally go to support the overall budget. We would prefer that the agency retain its independence, but be separate from the Fed and funded through the normal appropriations process. Earmarking Fed profits for particular purposes sets a bad precedent from the standpoint of accountability, as does a system in which the Fed's name is on policies it doesn't control.

The common thread of each of these options is an end to sectoral fragmentation through the consolidation of authority and responsibility.

#11: Subsidies for Nonproductive Investment, Taxes for Productive Investment

"When you build a new housing subdivision, you provide jobs for a few months. When you build a new factory, you provide jobs for years."

Ron Vara

One of the central themes of this book is that we need to fix chronic structural imbalances in our GDP Growth Drivers equation. One of the biggest and most important imbalances is underinvestment in productive capital such as new factories, plants, and equipment. One big way we could address this issue—and simultaneously help prevent a repeat of the housing bubble and more robust long-term growth—is to change our tax code.

Right now, it is a pernicious artifact of that tax code that we encourage too much investment in relatively nonproductive capital projects such as residential housing through the mortgage interest rate deduction. At the same time, we discourage investment in productive capital by heavily taxing investment in new factories, plants, and equipment through high marginal corporate income tax rates and high individual income tax rates on capital gains, dividends, and interest income. The Obama administration's tax policies magnify this problem.

We understand that homeownership is a sacred cow of the American political fabric. However, we also believe that it is long past time to revisit our policies on the mortgage interest rate deduction. As Robert Pozen wrote:

> "Most Americans agree that mortgage interest on their primary residence should be tax-deductible. However, the United States goes much further than other countries in tax deductions for mortgage interest. Interest deductions are available for mortgages on second homes, as well as for mortgages on a number of homes acquired by speculators hoping to sell or flip them quickly for a profit."[10]

Today, taxpayers can deduct the interest on mortgages worth up to a total of $1 million on their first and second homes. To begin reform, we need to do away with the mortgage interest rate deduction. Rather, we can simply limit the deduction to a family's primary residence and disallow such deductions for second homes. In offering this proposal, we agree with Roger Lowenstein that "tax policy was never intended to function as a price support. Even less should it support a putative housing bubble."[11]

This reform is nontrivial. Mortgage interest rate deductions cost the Treasury more than $75 billion a year. As a final comment, in the interests of equity, any such reform should be implemented only prospectively—that is, for any second homes bought in the future.

The New Law as the End of the Beginning

In Agatha Christie's thriller *And Then There Were None*, a murder in a grand mansion startles the other guests. Eventually they calm down—until the next murder strikes. As we write this, both Washington and Wall Street have slipped into complacency between the events of September 2008 and the still-dangerous environment of late-2010. The passage of the new financial reform law—its more than 2,300 pages notwithstanding—doesn't change the situation much. The case for financial regulatory reform we've outlined here remains strong, and basic building blocks of regulatory reform appear in many thoughtful proposals for change around the world. What remains is the challenge and opportunity of "acting in time," as in other areas we have emphasized in this book.

The time for real financial regulatory reform is now. A clear road map for reducing systemic risk, enhancing transparency, and modernizing regulatory institutions such as we have offered is better medicine than the new law.

Unfortunately, our political leaders have shown little interest in substantive reform. We can't just give Wall Street a slap on the wrist, as some suggest. But we also can't impose burdensome regulations without costs to millions of savers and borrowers as the new law has done.

In closing, we reiterate that although we need new regulation in some previously unregulated areas, the crisis has shown that the most precarious sectors of our financial system are those *already* subject to a great deal of regulation—regulation that has proven woefully ineffective. When our leaders choose to debate effective reform, new or revised regulations must be based on solid principles—chief among them the reduction of systemic risk.

Finally, we absolutely must have a U.S. financial regulatory structure that can achieve these goals. And the new law does not leave us in that position. Simply put, the regulatory structure must be entirely reorganized to become more integrated and efficient. Returning to the president's observation with which we opened this chapter, we must understand the crisis. The president and Congress have wasted an opportunity—but we can start a serious conversation now.

THE SCOPE OF THE CRISIS

Much has been written about the origins and consequences of the housing bubble. Rather than reprise these events in our main narrative, we offer this brief summary of what transpired and where we are now.

Clearly, we are facing the most serious financial crisis since the Great Depression. This crisis has manifested itself in credit losses, writedowns, liquidity shocks, deflated property values, and a contraction of the real economy. As of April 2009, the International Monetary Fund estimated total near-term global losses on U.S. credit-related debt to be $2.7 trillion.

The financial crisis of 2007–2009 and its aftermath have complex origins, but those origins share a four-letter word: *r-i-s-k*. The mispricing of risk, with inflationary consequences for asset prices in the boom and a downward spiral of collapsing asset prices and economic activity in the bust, must be central to economic and policy analysis of the crisis. Underlying factors in the undertow that drew the economy out to crisis seas are those we have discussed before. They include global saving and investment imbalances that contributed to low real interest rates and risk premiums in international capital markets for many years, a U.S. monetary policy that was too expansionary in the 2003–2005 period, and significant gaps in regulation in theory and practice.

The sharp contraction in the U.S. GDP during the 2007–2009 "Great Recession" can be directly traced to the adverse effects of the crisis on household consumption and business investment. Costs directly attributable to the crisis include new spending by the federal government, including the Troubled Assets Relief Program (originally $700 billion with smaller ultimate losses) and the stimulus package passed in February 2009 ($787 billion).

In the housing sector, banks took advantage of low interest rates and securitization opportunities to institute relaxed lending standards that drove mortgage lending throughout the early part of the decade to unprecedented heights. In fact, although the number of households in the United States increased only marginally between 1990 and 2008, the aggregate mortgage debt outstanding more than quadrupled during that same period. Increased borrowing by U.S. households was partially offset by climbing asset prices.

Of course, as we now know, the period of rising property values came to a close after reaching a peak in the second quarter of 2006. Home prices eventually fell by a third by the end of 2008. This bursting of the housing bubble virtually eliminated construction and sales activity for a period of time.

Today, American homeowners remain in trouble, with the percentage of delinquent mortgages at an all-time high. Moreover, more than 20% of all mortgages are in a negative equity position.

Although the situation is improving, the financial sector still faces pockets of instability. During the past two years, some of the most prominent banks and other financial institutions have failed or been acquired, bailed out, or placed in conservatorship.

The wreckage on Wall Street and elsewhere stems in part from the explosive growth in complex and mispriced mortgage-related securities. From 2001 to 2003, total residential mortgage-backed security (RMBS) issuance doubled, going from $1.3 trillion to $2.7 trillion. As the RMBS market cooled, the CDO market took off. Global issuance of CDOs—resecuritizations of other forms of debt—more than tripled in the two-year period between 2005 and 2007. As the housing bubble burst, the market for these securities dried up, and their values have plummeted.

Shrinking balance sheets and shaken confidence in the financial sector have in turn weakened the demand for other types of debt, such as corporate bonds and commercial paper. At the same time, the price of insuring bank debt through CDSs has skyrocketed, reflecting investors' skepticism toward the creditworthiness of banks. Forced to shrink their balance sheets to satisfy regulatory capital requirements, banks have constrained lending. The result continues to be problematic for businesses and consumers seeking loans.

Endnotes

1. President Barack Obama. Speech at Cooper Union. New York. April 22, 2010.

2. "A Larger Down Payment Means Greater Savings." TD Canada Trust Web site. http://www.tdcanadatrust.com/mortgages/downpayment.jsp.

3. "WaMu built a 'mortgage time bomb.'" *Los Angeles Times*. April 13, 2010.

4. "The Exploding ARM." November 1, 2007. http://www. bankruptcylawnetwork.com/2007/11/01/exploding-arm/.

5. Scott Patterson. "The Minds Behind the Meltdown." *Wall Street Journal*. January 22, 2010. Based on the book of the same name.

6. "Goldman Sachs Sued by the SEC for Fraud Tied to CDOs." *Bloomberg News*. April 16, 2010.

7. Robert Pozen. *Too Big to Save*. John Wiley & Sons, 2010. p. 72.

8. The other form of risk for bondholders is interest rate risk, which is the sum that bondholders regularly hedge. Bondholders should have the same opportunity to hedge default risk.

9. "The Myth of Too Big to Fail." *The American Prospect*. October 28, 2009.

10. Robert Pozen, p. 23.

11. Roger Lowenstein. "Who Needs the Mortgage-Interest Deduction?" *New York Times*. March 5, 2006.

chapter eleven

How to Implement Our Seeds of Prosperity Policy Blueprint

> *"To avoid large and unsustainable budget deficits, the nation will ultimately have to choose among higher taxes, modifications to entitlement programs such as Social Security and Medicare, less spending on everything else from education to defense, or some combination of the above. These choices are difficult, and it always seems easier to put them off—until the day they cannot be put off any more."*
>
> Ben Bernanke (April 2010)[1]

This warning from Federal Reserve Chairman Ben Bernanke gets it half right—but also half wrong.

Mr. Bernanke is right that if the profligate policies of Congress and the Obama administration continue in their current direction, we as a country will be caught between a proverbial rock and some hard choices. But where his advice goes off course is to offer as the only choice harsh budget and program cuts and painfully higher taxes. There is a better way—and it is embodied in the basic message of this book.

As we have explained, the best way to restore America's prosperity is to ensure a robust rate of long-term economic growth commensurate with our full potential GDP growth rate. The way to achieve this is to undertake the set of broad-based structural reforms that we have identified in our Seeds of Prosperity policy blueprint.

In identifying these reforms, we have used our GDP Growth Drivers equation and Ten Levers of Growth to illustrate how a wide range of fiscal, monetary, tax, trade, health care, and regulatory policies have led to the large structural imbalances that are keeping our economy from realizing its potential. These structural imbalances, with which you should now be very familiar, include overconsumption, underinvestment, excess government spending, and chronic trade imbalances.

As we have also pointed out, these structural imbalances have caused our economy to grow at a rate below its historical average over the past decade. This growth deficit has led to a loss of almost ten million jobs that could have been created. Moreover during this time, the growth in real average median household income has failed to keep up with the pace of previous decades.

Our Seeds of Prosperity policy blueprint seeks to reverse this economic stagnation, thereby avoiding the "rock and hard choices" trap. It does so through a suite of policies designed to rebalance our economy and put us on the path toward long-term prosperity.

This concluding chapter summarizes our blueprint. Our hope is that you, dear reader, will carry this message to your elected representatives. In so doing, you can help press the case for a "middle ground" policy strategy that will give us the best chance of political consensus and economic success.

Our Seeds of Destruction Problem

Chronic structural imbalances in the U.S. economy have led to a decade of economic growth significantly below our potential GDP growth rate, stagnant wages for many, and unacceptably high levels of unemployment.

Our Seeds of Prosperity Solution

To reach our full potential GDP growth rate in a sustainable fashion over the long term, we must rebalance our economy according to the principles of our Ten Levers of Growth and the insights gained from our analysis of the U.S. GDP Growth Drivers equation. Such a rebalancing will require a set of reforms in the areas of monetary and fiscal policy, tax and trade policy, energy policy, entitlements, health care, and financial regulation.

Recasting Monetary Policy

The Federal Reserve's easy monetary policies over the past decade have played a role and fueling a housing bubble in America's structural imbalance of overconsumption.

The Fed must turn its emphasis away from discretionary fine-tuning and firmly embrace a policy that has as its goals price stability and sustainable long-term growth.

The Fed must also fiercely guard its independence from both the White House and Capitol Hill and not succumb to the "political cycle" of easy money creation.

Rethinking the Use of a Fiscal Stimulus

We must wean ourselves from the idea that we can stimulate our way to prosperity. Instead, we must embrace the principle that only through structural reforms will we return to the path of long-term prosperity.

To avoid the debilitating effects of the structural imbalance of excessive government spending, we must shy away from further use of discretionary fiscal stimulus while having the patience to allow automatic stabilizers to do their job.

If a further fiscal stimulus is deemed to be absolutely necessary, it should strictly meet the test of being temporary, timely, and targeted.

Over the longer term, in implementing any stimulus, we should favor tax cuts to stimulate business investment over increased government expenditures. This way is the best one to stimulate job creation over both the short and longer term.

We must make our government more effective while limiting both its size and the size of our budget deficits and national debt, as well as Americans' tax burden. At present, we are going in exactly the opposite direction of all these goals.

Unburdening Our Tax Policy

America's complex income-based tax system reinforces all four major structural imbalances in the U.S. economy. It discourages both saving and investment while handcuffing American exporters. This limitation occurs even as Washington's enormous power to tax promotes a cult of fiscal irresponsibility within the myopic confines of the Beltway. However, the American economy will never return to full prosperity until it completes a very broad-based tax reform.

The failure to engage in broad-based tax reform reflects a failure of both Democrats and Republicans to escape ideological straitjackets. Many Democrats have fallen in love with taxing both "the rich" and "big business," oblivious to the growth-stalling effects of onerous taxes on savings, investment, entrepreneurship, and job creation. Many Republicans advocate cutting taxes in the current broken system rather than acknowledge the need for a certain level of government revenues and bold reforms.

Any broad-based tax reform should seek to broaden the tax base, reduce marginal tax rates, and, most important from a growth-stimulating perspective, remove any tax incentives against savings, investment, entrepreneurial risk-taking, and exports.

One approach examined by President George W. Bush's Advisory Panel integrates a consumption tax component into our current income tax structure. This "blended" approach cuts in half the number of tax brackets, reduces the highest marginal tax rate, and reduces the tax rate on dividends, capital gains, and interest. For businesses, it also allows expensing for all new investment and removes the deductibility for interest payments, while providing for border tax adjustments.

Although this blended approach does not eliminate the double taxation of capital income or the biases against savings and investment, it would significantly increase savings and capital formation and the economic and wage growth that come with it.

An even more effective approach that we favor extends the blended approach to reward saving and capital investment more completely. For individuals, income would continue to be taxed with a progressive rate structure. However, all forms of capital income earned by individuals—interest, dividends, and capital gains—would be exempt. For businesses, corporate profits would likewise continue to be taxed. However, all capital investment would be fully expensed.

From an economic point of view, such a "progressive consumption tax" meets the most important challenge of stimulating growth by providing maximum incentives for individual saving and business investment while removing the double taxation of capital income.

From a political point of view, this approach represents a "middle ground" reform. Democrats can support it because it maintains the progressivity of the current income tax structure. Republicans can likewise support it because it is fiscally neutral and represents a far more efficient form of taxation.

Freeing Our Trade Policy from Mercantilist and Protectionist Chains

Given that America's chronic trade deficits act as a brake on growth and raise difficult issues related to a loss of America's political sovereignty, it is critical that they be reduced.

If we want to reduce America's large and chronic trade deficits, there are only two major ways to do so—by reducing America's heavy oil import dependence, and by shrinking America's trade imbalance, particularly with China.

China engages in a wide range of protectionist and mercantilist practices that make it very difficult for American businesses to compete on a level, free-trade playing field and equally difficult for the United States to reduce its trade deficit with China. For these reasons, America's best chance of reducing its non-oil-related trade deficit lies with constructive trade reform with China.

Because free trade is one of the most important of the Ten Levers of Growth, both the president and Congress must emphasize that free trade means full compliance with WTO rules. By compliance, we mean not relying on any illegal export subsidies or currency manipulation and ensuring the presence of strong protection of intellectual property, strict prohibitions against forced technology transfer, reasonable environmental and health and safety standards that meet international norms, free and open access to each country's domestic markets, and an unrestricted global market in raw materials.

A key reason China has been able to run a large trade surplus with the United States is America's extremely low saving rate. Boosting the American saving rate should be part of our national economic overall trade policy.

The Soft, Hard, and Smart Paths to Greater Energy Independence

America has 4.5% of the world's population and possesses less than 3% of proven world oil reserves. But we consume almost 25% of annual world oil production and depend on foreign imports for 65% of our oil needs.

This "oil addiction" reduces our GDP growth rate by helping stall three of the main drivers of our GDP equation—consumption, investment, and net exports. If America truly wants to return to its full potential GDP growth rate, we must significantly reduce our oil import dependence.

Complete energy independence (or "autarky") is neither feasible nor desirable. However, reducing our dependence on foreign oil to a level more consistent with economic prosperity and national security clearly is. We believe there is at least one simple but highly effective market-driven, middle-ground solution that both Democrats and Republicans can embrace.

Many Democrats prefer to solve our energy problems using "soft-path" options ranging from energy conservation and regulatory fixes such as higher gas mileage standards to a greater reliance on renewables such as solar and wind. In contrast, many Republicans prefer "hard-path" options ranging from drilling for more oil and developing more domestic natural gas to the increased use of coal and nuclear power.

We believe that the truly "smart path" to reducing our oil independence lies in embracing both hard and soft path options. Our "Law of Oil Import Substitution" states that as the price of imported oil rises, America's import dependence falls as both soft and hard path oil substitutes become more economically attractive. This law leads us to our market-driven policy solution:

To bring more domestic soft and hard path oil substitutes into the market, we propose an oil price floor. To set this floor, the White House, in conjunction with the U.S. Congress and the Department of Energy, first determines the desired target rate of oil use and import reduction. To achieve this targeted reduction, the target price floor is set by imposing a *flexible* fee. This fee is equal to the difference between the actual world price for a barrel of oil and the target price necessary to achieve the desired reduction in oil use and import dependence.

Such a *flexible* fee is quite different from the kind of *permanent* taxes on oil imports (and gasoline) that have frequently been proposed. It is levied *only* when the world price of oil falls below the target level. As the world price of oil moves toward the target price, the fee is *reduced*. Moreover, whenever the world price of oil rises above the target level, the fee is *removed*, and the desired level of oil use and import reduction is achieved purely through market forces.

This market-based flexibility makes our proposed oil price floor a far more politically palatable solution than any permanent tax on either oil imports or gasoline. Neither of these has broad support among the general public.

We also believe that any revenues raised from such a fee should be returned to the American people in the form of tax cuts—thereby making the foreign oil tax revenue-neutral.

Democrats can embrace such an approach because it fulfills the goals of promoting both energy conservation and environmental stewardship and the development of alternative energy sources. Its flexible nature likewise reduces concerns about the regressivity of such a fee and any transient negative impacts on the poor.

Republicans can embrace such a proposal because it is market-driven, revenue-neutral, and applied only when the price of oil rises above the target. It also removes the need for any elaborate regulatory programs such as fuel efficiency standards for cars. Furthermore, it removes the need to heavily subsidize any of a number of import substitutes—whether corn-based ethanol, coal-to-liquid synfuels, or renewables.

(Truly) Saving Social Security

America's three largest entitlement programs—Social Security, Medicare, and Medicaid—face looming funding deficits that will threaten their very existence and the nation's fiscal health over time. Despite this looming crisis, our political leaders continue to expand America's entitlement programs rather than rein them in—for example, the Bush Medicare drug bill in 2003 and ObamaCare in 2010.

By our Iron Law of Entitlement Reform, any attempt to close the looming entitlement spending gap by further raising taxes, running large budget deficits, or cutting spending on critical needs such as education and infrastructure will backfire. The result will be less innovation and entrepreneurship, slower economic growth, lower wages, fewer people employed, less tax revenue collected, and an even larger budget deficit.

Two policy options, working in combination, have the potential to close all, or almost all, of the forecast spending gap for Social Security.

First, we should raise the retirement age to better match rising life expectancies—but we should do so in a gradual and orderly fashion, as a matter of equity. The argument for this is self-evident. When Social Security was established in 1935, the retirement age was set at 65—roughly the same as the life expectancy of the average American. Today, average life expectancy has risen to close to 80, yet the retirement age has been raised to only 67.

Second, we should index initial Social Security benefits to prices rather than wages so as to maintain real, inflation-adjusted purchasing power for beneficiaries. Because wages have historically risen significantly faster than prices, the current method of wage indexing amounts to an extra boost in purchasing power for retirees. However, this boost has not been properly funded by the payroll taxes that retirees and their employers have paid into the system.

Price indexing is a fair way to address this problem because it does not result in any loss in real purchasing power by beneficiaries. Instead, by the very definition of price indexing, benefits keep pace with the rate of inflation. In this way, the real purchasing power and standard of living of retirees are preserved.

This combination of raising the retirement age and moving to a price-indexing system would close most or even all of the Social Security spending gap. And we can use some of the savings to strengthen benefits for low-income individuals. This combination would do so with the least damage to our economy and in a way that would guarantee greater intergenerational equity and thereby reduce inaction due to future political conflict.

More Focus and Flexibility for Medicare and Medicaid

The most important way to stop Medicare and Medicaid from devouring an ever-larger share of America's economic pie is to bring health care costs under control. We can also make at least some progress by targeting Medicare and Medicaid spending more at lower-income households.

For Medicaid, flexibility is the key. A more flexible approach means moving to a block-grant-type structure in which the federal government annually gives each state the Medicaid funding it received the year before, adjusted for inflation and for changes in the state's population of low-income individuals—with few or no strings attached.

For Medicare, the watchwords are cost-consciousness and focus. Cost-consciousness means setting an explicit annual budget for Medicare. This alternative is preferable to our current "mandatory" spending frame of mind, which is simply inconsistent with the productivity enhancements and cost control we need.

To focus Medicare better, we must also move away from the current fee-for-service reimbursement system. Instead, Medicare could give each retiree support for a basic health plan, which individuals could supplement at their own expense. Support should focus on lower-income individuals, with much less assistance for more affluent seniors.

Starting Over on Health Care

Even though America spends almost twice as much per person on health care as many other major industrial countries, the quality of our health care lags behind most other countries. We can measure this by yardsticks as disparate as infant mortality, survival rates for major diseases, and deaths due to medical error.

President Barack Obama was right to pursue health care reform. America's costly health care system doesn't deliver enough value for the money spent. However, the legislation he slipped through Congress is just plain wrong.

The primary thrust of ObamaCare is to expand health insurance coverage rather than containing costs. This new and massive entitlement will be paid for in the two worst possible ways—by further increasing the budget deficit and by further raising taxes. The inevitable consequences will be to exacerbate our health care cost problem while stalling the economy.

Because health care costs are rising so fast, politicians inevitably turn to raising taxes to finance programs such as Medicare and Medicaid. For example, under ObamaCare, the Medicare payroll tax will jump from 1.45% to 2.35% for upper-income filers. ObamaCare will also slap a 3.8% tax onto capital gains, interest income, and dividends starting in 2013. These tax hikes will depress and thereby slow down the rate of innovation, job creation, and wage growth.

There is a clear market-driven path toward reducing health care costs while improving medical care quality. Moving down this path will require individuals to take much greater responsibility for their health care. Also, health insurers and health care providers must face more fully the competitive forces in the marketplace.

The three market-driven policy changes described next go a long way toward achieving the objectives of lower-cost and higher-quality care.

Eliminate the Tax Code Bias for Employer-Provided Insurance

Under today's employer-provided insurance system, neither employers nor employees pay income or payroll taxes on the employer's contribution to an employee's insurance plan. These tax preferences create large incentives for employees to purchase much more expensive employer-provided insurance plans with low deductibles and low copayment rates rather than "true insurance" plans geared primarily toward covering catastrophic health events.

Within this system, $5 out of every $6 of health care spending is paid for by someone other than the person receiving care—insurance companies, employers, or the government. The resultant price insensitivity of consumers leads to a whole range of wasteful medical practices and the overconsumption of low-value-added health care services.

Eliminating one of America's most enduring and lucrative tax preferences is a huge political hot potato. Given this high hurdle, we propose a more palatable "second-best" way to address the clear bias toward employer-provided health plans. All health spending could be tax-deductible—including out-of-pocket payments, purchases of individual insurance, and purchases of COBRA coverage.

Such deductibility mitigates the tax bias against individual insurance, because both employer-sponsored and individual insurance can be acquired with pre-income tax dollars. The tax change also enhances the fairness of the federal income tax system. Ultimately, allowing health care expenses to be tax-deductible should help reduce the growth in health costs, because greater cost consciousness leads to less spending.

Remove State Barriers

"Mandated benefits laws" in some states require health plans to cover particular types of persons, services, or providers such as chiropractors. But such mandates increase health insurance costs by at least 5%, and possibly as much as 15%, by muting market signals. They should be repealed.

"Any willing provider" laws in some states require health plans to accept bills from any doctor, hospital, or pharmacist who is willing to accept the plan's terms and conditions. Studies indicate such laws likewise increase costs by 1% to 2% by weakening the cost-containment effects of managed-care plans. Likewise, they should be repealed.

State-by-state regulation also raises costs by reducing competition among insurance companies and by allowing state legislatures to impose insurance mandates that raise prices while preventing residents from getting policies more suitable for their needs. Individuals should, however, be allowed to buy health insurance offered in states other than those in which they live or in a national market. This change would increase competition and lower insurance prices.

Reform Malpractice Laws

Our system of excessive litigation leads to higher costs and fewer choices for patients because of "defensive medicine." Ironically, it also leads to more, rather than fewer, medical errors by systematically suppressing the collection and analysis of precisely the kind of hospital and patient data that would otherwise help reduce medical errors.

We propose a reasonable national cap on noneconomic damages in medical malpractice lawsuits. This would go a long way toward reducing costs and decreasing unnecessary defensive medicine.

We also propose limiting the discoverability of data in legal proceedings that have been collected for the purposes of improving quality and reducing medical errors. Such legal protection will encourage health care organizations to develop policies to collect and analyze information about medical errors. It also will encourage doctors, nurses, and other health care workers to report mistakes. Passing such legislation would be an important step toward reducing medical errors.

Likewise, we believe that both patients and health care providers should be given more freedom to experiment with alternatives to litigation such as alternative dispute resolution. This form of arbitration would replace the current "compensation lottery" with a more consistent decision-making process.

*　　*　　*

The three types of health care reform policies we propose offer considerable advantages over ObamaCare. Instead of raising health care costs, they fundamentally change incentives among individuals, insurers, and providers to gradually slow the growth in costs by reducing inefficient demand without sacrificing quality and innovation. Instead of radically changing health care overnight, they take an incremental approach, respecting the tremendous uncertainty surrounding the effectiveness of different approaches to rein in costs.

Preventing Another Housing Bubble and Financial Crisis

It was not "too little regulation" that caused the financial crisis. Instead, the lack of *effective* regulation in the face of a set of overwhelmingly powerful perverse incentives led astray many actors in the housing bubble drama. Failing to understand this—and failing to understand that the primary goal of financial regulation should be to reduce the likelihood of crises—has resulted in yet another massive piece of legislation by the Obama administration that widely misses the mark.

As with ObamaCare, this legislation represents a significant expansion of the government bureaucracy. It establishes no fewer than five new government agencies and entities even as it fails to reduce the chance of "too big to fail" bailouts. Following an Occam's Razor approach, we offer a much simpler and more direct route to reform based on an analysis of the causes of the 2007–2009 crisis.

#1: Better Monetary Policy

The U.S. housing bubble and its recessionary aftermath were made worse by easy money policies of the U.S. Federal Reserve. One of the best ways to avoid a reoccurrence is for the Fed to adopt a less accommodative and more monetary policy in economic recoveries and be more cognizant of the affects of its actions on financial stability.

#2: More Money Down

Because many homeowners had little or no equity in their homes, it was far too easy for them to simply walk away when the bubble burst.

To avoid this problem of "no skin in the game," we should adopt a variation of the successful Canadian model: Homeowners should be required to put down at least 20% as a down payment—or purchase mortgage loan insurance.

#3: An End to Exotic Mortgages

The proliferation of a wide range of exotic subprime mortgage lending instruments—from adjustable-rate mortgages and balloon mortgages to interest-only loans and "liar loans"—allowed people who could not afford to buy a house to do just that. We do not need to create a huge Consumer Protection bureaucracy to solve this problem, as the new financial reform law has done. Rather, we need to prohibit or restrict high-risk mortgage products and lending practices.

#4: More Transparency for Fannie Mae and Freddie Mac

In the 2007–2009 crisis, flawed mathematical models grossly underestimated risk and worked in conjunction with a host of new and equally exotic financial instruments such as mortgage-backed securities (MBSs). This led to bailouts of government-sponsored entities such as Fannie Mae and Freddie Mac. One clear lesson is that it is inappropriate for these government-sponsored entities to allow their shareholders to benefit from high risk-taking while taxpayers are forced to bail them out. If we are to have a public presence in the housing market, it should be transparent, and the firms should hedge their balance sheet risk. However, the Obama administration and new financial reform law offer little guidance here.

#5: Improving the Credit Rating Agencies

A second type of exotic instrument—the collateralized debt obligation (CDO)—helped lead to the collapse of Wall Street icons such as Bear Stearns and Lehman Brothers. Despite the high risk, CDO investors were told by supposedly reputable credit agencies such as Dun & Bradstreet, Fitch, Moody's Investor Service, and Standard & Poor's that their CDO securities were "investment grade."

We must ensure more accurate credit ratings and far greater disclosure of just exactly what information credit ratings are based on—particularly for structured finance securities. CRAs therefore should be required to make extensive disclosure of the criteria, methodologies, models, processes, key assumptions, and scenario analyses they employ in rating all types of securities. Despite some positive features of the new financial reform law in these areas, it encourages litigation instead of urging the SEC to do its job.

#6: A Centralized Clearinghouse for Derivatives

Collateralized debt obligations played a key role in the collapse of the housing bubble and the ensuing financial crisis (as well as the AIG bailout). However, they would not have done nearly as much damage without the existence of another exotic lending instrument—the credit default swap (CDS). Because CDS derivatives are important tools for both measuring and diversifying credit risk, they should not be banned, as many critics have called for. Rather, the focus should be on reducing systemic risk, which is the risk of collapse of an entire system or entire market, exacerbated by links and interdependencies.

The best way to do so is through a "centralized clearinghouse." Such a clearinghouse would enhance the liquidity and transparency of the CDS market by actively managing daily collateral requirements of clearinghouse members and the netting of positions between and among them. Yes, the Treasury Department has pledged to subject all standardized OTC derivative contracts—particularly CDSs. But thus far, it has exercised little leadership in centralized clearing.

#7: More Flexible Bank Capital Reserves

By providing a cushion against losses, capital reserves are supposed to act as a first line of defense against bank failures and their knock-on consequences for systemic risk. One of the most important flaws of the current regulatory framework for setting minimum capital levels is that reserve levels are fixed rather than flexible over the course of the business cycle. This inflexibility forces banks to raise capital in a business cycle downturn, and as losses mount, capital levels are depleted. The result is that any contraction in the economy is further amplified by an increasing inability of the banks to lend.

We propose a shift to business-cycle-sensitive capital require-ments to avoid a boom-bust cycle from inflexible capital limits. One way to do this is to require financial institutions to build up reserves during booms. A second alternative is to raise contingent capital dur-ing a downturn by converting unsecured debt to equity. In addition, because large or important institutions pose systemic risks, they should be required to hold a larger capital buffer.

#8: Eliminating "Too Big to Fail"

As the failure of Lehman and the rescue of AIG indicated, we have had significant trouble resolving the failure of big, complicated finan-cial institutions. This brick in the wall of "too big to fail" must be replaced. Otherwise, we will repeat the destructive process of massive bailouts that we witnessed during the last crisis.

The Obama Treasury has proposed the creation of an additional insolvency regime with powers similar to those available for banks that can be invoked when a financial company's insolvency poses a systemic risk to market. However, the Treasury's proposals are inadequate. A better alternative is the implementation of a comprehensive Financial Company Resolution Act, applicable to all financial institutions.

The new financial reform law, while too big to read, offers little to deal with the elephant in the room of too-big-to-fail. While the law tackles resolution authority, it lacks key specifics. (At least the law jettisoned the Obama administration's call to capitalize a large "orderly liquidation fund" in advance; this was an open invitation to bailouts.)

#9: Replacing a Fragmented and Sectoral Regulatory Model

Most other leading financial center countries have moved toward consolidated financial oversight. But the United States remains saddled with a fragmented and sectoral model of regulation. This model was woefully unprepared to deal with the 2007–2009 financial crisis and all the problems of widespread systemic risk it entails. The clear lesson from the crisis—and the exceedingly slow reaction times of our key but fragmented regulatory institutions—is that effective financial regulation going forward will inevitably require a reorganization of the current regulatory structure.

The new financial reform law vests systemic risk regulation in an interagency council composed of several existing regulatory agencies, but this approach is likely to fail in preventing crises. This important role should be retained by the Federal Reserve for the simple but powerful reason that one regulator, and one regulator alone, needs both the authority and accountability to regulate matters pertaining to systemic risk.

We also propose a new U.S. Financial Services Authority (USFSA) that would regulate all aspects of the financial system, including market structure and activities and safety and soundness for all financial institutions. (It also might possibly regulate consumer and investor protection with respect to financial products if this responsibility were lodged with the USFSA.)

The new law's placement of a Consumer Protection Agency in the Fed is cynical. Its primary purpose is to obtain off-balance-sheet Fed funding from the profits the Fed makes from monetary policy and other services (over $50 billion in 2009). Earmarking Fed profits for particular purposes sets a bad precedent from the standpoint of accountability, as does a system in which the Fed's name is on policies it doesn't control.

#10: Curtailing Subsidies for Nonproductive Investment

One of the central themes of this book is that we need to fix chronic structural imbalances in our GDP Growth Drivers equation. Unfortunately, the current tax code encourages too much investment in relatively nonproductive capital projects such as residential housing through the mortgage interest rate deduction. It also *discourages* investment in productive capital through high marginal corporate income tax rates and high individual income tax rates on capital gains, dividends, and interest income.

Although we understand that homeownership is a sacred cow of the American political fabric, we also believe that it is long past time to revisit our policies on the mortgage interest rate deduction. Our proposal is not to do away with the mortgage interest rate deduction. Rather, it is to limit the deduction to a family's primary residence and disallow such deductions for second homes. And Congress and the president should advance the cause of tax reform to reduce the costly tax bias against business investment.

Conclusion

We wrote this book because we are deeply concerned about our country's economic future. Our concern stems from the inability of so many of our leaders to understand this simple truth:

Improvements in the American economy, like the economies of all nations of the world, depend on growth in income. This growth comes from increases in standards of living and is driven by four components: consumption, business investment, government spending, and net exports. Business investment and net exports are particularly important in terms of providing the innovation, increased productivity, job creation, and long-term growth that we need to be a prosperous nation. Because the Washington establishment fails to understand this simple truth, it continues to adopt more and more onerous tax and regulatory policies that suppress business investment while bloating our government, discouraging savings, and destroying the competitive advantages we need to boost our export trade.

Our leaders have often sidestepped important, difficult reforms. Instead, we have been treated to policies that encourage consumption—even if that consumption is unsustainable—instead of policies that will raise all our incomes and secure our future. We deserve better than this from our political elites. And our children and their children also deserve much better.

This book has described a better way that will shift us from the current "Seeds of Destruction" agenda in which we are now engaged onto the path of our Seeds of Prosperity blueprint.

The message will be heard only if, after reading this book, you also speak out—and urge our political leaders to understand what this country needs to build a strong economy and act on it.

If not now, when?

Endnote

1. Ben Bernanke. Speech before the Dallas Regional Chamber. April 7, 2010. http://www.federalreserve.gov/newsevents/speech/20100407a.htm.

index

Q–R

U–V

Press

FINANCIAL TIMES

In an increasingly competitive world, it is quality
of thinking that gives an edge—an idea that opens new
doors, a technique that solves a problem, or an insight
that simply helps make sense of it all.

We work with leading authors in the various arenas
of business and finance to bring cutting-edge thinking
and best-learning practices to a global market.

It is our goal to create world-class print publications
and electronic products that give readers
knowledge and understanding that can then be
applied, whether studying or at work.

To find out more about our business
products, you can visit us at www.ftpress.com.